# THE GOSPEL ACCORDING TO JOHN

# The Gospel According to
# JOHN

*With Notes
by Craig Munro*

RITCHIE
John Ritchie Publishing

40 Beansburn, Kilmarnock, Scotland

# Contents

# The Gospel According to John

This book presents the "gospel of Jesus Christ, the Son of God". The Apostle John leaves us in no doubt why He wrote this Gospel: "**these [*things*] are written, that you might believe that Jesus is the Christ, the Son of God; and that believing ye might have life through His name**" (John 20.31). This gospel, therefore, is designed to introduce the reader to the eternal Son of God Who is willing to give everyone eternal life, upon the basis of faith.

The word 'Gospel' simply means good news and there are four gospel accounts of the life of Christ in the Bible – Matthew, Mark, Luke and John. The Bible itself is an amazing book. It is actually a library of sixty-six books written originally in three languages, on three continents and over a period of 1500 years, by kings, commoners, priests and prisoners. Amazingly the message of each book is consistent with the whole. They tell us of the greatness of God and His desire to bless mankind. We hope that after reading one of the books of the Bible you will want to read them all.

The four gospels together provide a very full picture of the person and work of the Lord Jesus Christ. They are, however, not carbon copies of each other. Matthew the converted tax collector tends to concentrate on proving to a Jewish audience that Christ was the Messiah, the Son of David, the true King. Mark sets out to prove that the Lord Jesus Christ was God's perfect Servant, emphasising the actions of Christ and the tireless energy that the Lord Jesus exerted in His full and perfect service down here on earth. Doctor Luke stresses to a Gentile audience the perfect, holy, loving manhood of Christ. John, the fisherman, selects and describes for us a number of individuals who were initially unbelievers but came to believe that Jesus is the Son of God and through believing in Him obtained eternal life. John focuses particularly on the climax to His service on earth at the cross of Calvary with over half of the Gospel concentrating on the last few days before His death and resurrection. John does not want us to miss certain key facts about the Lord Jesus: the Lord Jesus is God and yet as a Man has fully revealed the true God to us; He has laid down His life voluntarily for the world and died for our sins; He has risen again victoriously on the third day and is alive to save all those who will repent of their sin and believe in Him for salvation. This Gospel is published with the prayer that you might receive Jesus Christ as your Lord and Saviour and receive eternal life. If you are already a Christian, this Gospel will also help you in your daily walk with God.

**Marginal Notes**

This Gospel is published with marginal notes for three reasons:
(1) This translation is the King James Version, first published in 1611. Some words need to be explained that are not in current use or that have changed their meaning.

(2) There are themes or thoughts that appear throughout the gospel. Marginal comments allow the reader to trace some of these themes, and then re-examine the context and setting of each reference.

(3) Some biblical illustrations are not automatically understandable to a modern western mind and require explanation. Marginal comments of this nature are not frequent, as we believe Scripture should speak for itself.

## Reflective Questions and Notes

A page with some reflective questions and a place to take notes is contained after the prologue (John 1.1-1.18) and at the end of each chapter. These pages are designed to provoke thought and to encourage the reader to pause, take notes and reflect in their personal daily readings, to facilitate discussion in small group bible studies, and for use in personal evangelism.

# John 3.16 – The Love of God

This verse (John 3.16) composed of only 25 words seems to encompass the whole gospel of Jesus Christ. It tells of the greatness of the love of God. Many have become true believers in the Lord Jesus Christ through this text alone. We hope that you will too.

> **For G**od so loved the World that He Gave His
> **O**nly Begotten
> **S**on that whosoever believeth in Him should not
> **P**erish but have
> **E**verlasting
> **L**ife

**His Love is without Reason – "For God so loved the world".** Why would God love a world that breaks his ten commandments and curses His Name daily? A world that has made gods in their own image: gods that smile on their sins and accommodate all their discrepancies but still blesses their weddings and funerals. Why would God love a world that lives their life without Him, a world that has mountains of food and yet starves millions, a world where there is ample wealth and yet kills and wars and maims humans for more power? Why would God love a world that has rejected, cruelly whipped, and crucified His Son? And yet He does. He is a holy God and cannot tolerate our sin but He loves us unconditionally. What a God! Dear reader you are loved of God no matter who you are or what you have done. His love is different to human love – it is without reason.

**His Love is without Restraint – "That He gave His only begotten Son".** His giving is beyond description. He gave His darling, His only beloved; the very best of heaven. He did not give us an angel or even an archangel but the eternal Son of God, the Creator of the Universe, was given for this wretched world and given for all of us. Incredibly, He was given to the death of a cross, given to pay the punishment of our sins in His own body on the tree.  There was nothing held back. He gave all. What love!

**His Love is without Restriction – "that whosoever".** Our love is partial – as humans we love those who love us. We find it hard to love the unlovely or those who do not love us back. But God loves the unlovely and His love is unrestricted; it goes out to the 'whosoever' – every boy, girl, man and woman. All can be saved. Christ died for all people and for all sins. No one is outside the scope of His love.

**His love is without Recompense – "believes in Him".**  It does not say 'achieve' it says 'believe'. He is not asking us to DO anything, the work is all DONE by the Lord Jesus when He died for our sins at Calvary and rose again. Salvation is not a payment for hard work but a free gift of grace to undeserving cases. All He requires is for us to believe in Him – that is believe on the Lord Jesus Christ for salvation. He does not ask us to believe **a religion** or a **church** – but come and have an eternal **relationship** with **Christ.**

**His Love is without Renewal - "should not perish but have everlasting life".** Most gifts eventually need replaced. His gift of love is everlasting. It never needs replaced. Human love is temperamental and can fluctuate. His gift of love is constant, never changing. When God makes a promise, He keeps it for all eternity. Those who receive the Lord Jesus Christ as Saviour are given everlasting life, they will also go to heaven. It is a promise from God whose love is eternal and whose Word is truth. You can trust Him.

**His Love can be Refused**
Like any gift, the gift of *God's love needs to be accepted*. He will never force His love upon you. He wants no conscripts. It has cost Him everything but He still wants you to voluntarily receive the gift of everlasting life. Do not miss this offer of His incredible love and tragically choose to face the punishment for your own sins eternally in hell. His love is a free gift and it is real and eternal but it has to be received. Repent of your sins and trust Him today. It will be the biggest life changing decision of your life and one you will never regret.

# John 1

## The Establishment of the Son's Titles and His First Disciples vv.1-51

### *The Word in Eternity and in Creation vv.1-5*

1 In the beginning was the Word, and the Word was with God, and the Word was God.

2 The same was in the beginning with God.

3 All things were made by him; and without him was not any thing made that was made.

4 In him was life; and the life was the light of men.

5 And the light shineth in darkness; and the darkness comprehended it not.

### *The Light of the World in the World vv.6-14*

6 There was a man sent from God, whose name was John.

7 The same came for a witness, to bear witness of the Light, that all men through him might believe.

8 He was not that Light, but was sent to bear witness of that Light.

9 That was the true Light, which lighteth every man that cometh into the world.

1.1 'The Word' is a title for the Lord Jesus Christ, the Son of God – see verse 14. 'The Word' in Greek is 'Logos' meaning that Christ is the One who is the full expression and revelation of God.

'Beginning" – The Word was already there in the beginning. He is eternal.

'Was God' – this is a definitive statement of the Christian faith. The Lord Jesus is God. This truth is known as the deity of Christ.

'With God' – The Lord Jesus 'is God' and is 'with God' emphasising fellowship and unity within the Godhead. There is one God but that one God is expressed in three persons – God the Father, God the Son and God the Holy Spirit (Matt. 28.19; 2 Cor. 13.14). This truth is known as the Trinity. Just as water is two hydrogen molecules and an oxygen molecule ($H_2O$) but can exist in three phases, water (liquid), ice (solid) and steam (gas) so the One God is revealed as The Father, Son and Holy Spirit.

1.3 'All things were made by Him' – there is an explanation to existence. He is the designer of the universe. Before there was 'matter' there was 'mind' (logos) and mind did not come from matter.

1.4 'Life and light' are key themes in this gospel. Christ will claim to be the 'bread of life' (John 6.35) and the 'light of the world'(John 8.12; 9.5).

1.5 'darkness comprehended it not" – the darkness speaks of evil in the Bible but the darkness could not extinguish the light of Christ.

1.6 This John is John the Baptist who heralded in the Christ, vv. 19-28.

10 He was in the world, and the world was made by him, and the world knew him not.

11 He came unto his own, and his own received him not.

12 But as many as received him, to them gave he power to become the sons of God, even to them that believe on his name:

13 Which were born, not of blood, nor of the will of the flesh, nor of the will of man, but of God.

14 And the Word was made flesh, and dwelt among us, (and we beheld his glory, the glory as of the only begotten of the Father,) full of grace and truth.

## *The Testimony of John the Baptist vv.15-28*

15 John bare witness of him, and cried, saying, This was he of whom I spake, He that cometh after me is preferred before me: for he was before me.

16 And of his fulness have all we received, and grace for grace.

17 For the law was given by Moses, but grace and truth came by Jesus Christ.

18 No man hath seen God at any time, the only begotten Son, which is in the bosom of the Father, he hath declared him.

1.10 The Lord Jesus came to Bethlehem and was unrecognized. The Creator was unknown and unwanted.

1.11 Literally this would read: 'He came unto His own things and His own people did not receive Him'. He was rejected by His own people.

1.12 – 'believe on His Name' – this is another key theme in John's Gospel. Believing on Christ is the basis of being born again and having salvation, everlasting life (John 3.18; 4.39,41,50; 6.29,64; 8.30; 12.11; 20.29, 31).

1.13 'not of blood' – new birth is not genetic, does not run in the blood;

'nor of the will of the flesh' – new birth is not through human effort and good works;

'nor of the will of man'- new birth is not through human reasoning or intellect;

'But of God' – God is the One who saves and makes people children in His family through belief (faith) in Christ.

1.14 – This is another key doctrine of the Christian faith. God became flesh (not into flesh). God became a real man. It is known as the incarnation of Christ. His humanity was different to any other person as it was sinless (full of grace and truth) but it was still real.

1.15 – 'preferred before me' means 'He has preference, priority' i.e. John is saying, 'He is greater than me';

'for He was before me'- John the Baptist was teaching that although the Christ was born after John, as God, He existed eternally. He was alive before John was ever born.

1.17 'the law (e.g. the ten commandments) came by Moses' – the law highlighted our sin and showed us the need of salvation and could bring about repentance but the law could not save us.

"Grace and truth"- came by Jesus Christ. The Lord Jesus still brought the sharp edge of truth to us about our sin but there was also grace to save us and cleanse us from sin.

1.18 The Lord Jesus has fully declared the Father to us. We who have never seen God have now seen him in the person of His Son.

A.  Who is "the Word"? vv.1,14,17,18.

B.  How is "the Word" described? vv.1,3,4,5,9.

C.  What does the Word reveal? vv.14,18.

D.  What happens if you receive Christ? vv.10-13.

______________________________________

______________________________________

______________________________________

______________________________________

______________________________________

19 And this is the record of John, when the Jews sent priests and Levites from Jerusalem to ask him, Who art thou?

20 And he confessed, and denied not; but confessed, I am not the Christ.

21 And they asked him, What then? Art thou Elias? And he saith, I am not. Art thou that prophet? And he answered, No.

22 Then said they unto him, Who art thou? that we may give an answer to them that sent us. What sayest thou of thyself?

23 He said, I am the voice of one crying in the wilderness, Make straight the way of the Lord, as said the prophet Esaias.

24 And they which were sent were of the Pharisees.

25 And they asked him, and said unto him, Why baptizest thou then, if thou be not that Christ, nor Elias, neither that prophet?

26 John answered them, saying, I baptize with water: but there standeth one among you, whom ye know not;

27 He it is, who coming after me is preferred before me, whose shoe's latchet I am not worthy to unloose.

28 These things were done in Bethabara beyond Jordan, where John was baptizing.

**John's Identification of the Son of God vv.29-34**

29 **The next day John seeth Jesus coming unto him, and saith, Behold the Lamb of God, which taketh away the sin of the world**.

30 This is he of whom I said, After me cometh a man which is preferred before me: for he was before me.

31 And I knew him not: but that he should be made manifest to Israel, therefore am I come baptizing with water.

32 And John bare record, saying, I saw the Spirit descending from heaven like a dove, and it abode upon him.

33 And I knew him not: but he that sent me to baptize with water, the same said unto me, Upon whom thou shalt see the Spirit descending, and remaining on him, the same is he which baptizeth with the Holy Ghost.

1.21 Elias means Elijah, a prophet found in 1 Kings 17 - 2 Kings 2.

1.23 This is a quotation from Isaiah 40, written over 700 years before John the Baptist was born. John knew He was not the Christ (Messiah) but he knew he was there to herald the Christ into the world.

1.24 Pharisees – a strict sect of the Jews.

1.27 'preferred before me' (see v15) means 'is greater than me'. John feels he is unworthy to even stoop down and unloose the buckle of the sandals of the Lord Jesus.

1.29 'The lamb of God' is a title of the Messiah. The question had been asked by Isaac thousands of years before, 'where is the Lamb?' (Gen 22. 7) and all lambs sacrificed for sins subsequently were unable to purge sins but simply pointed to the coming of the Messiah, the Lamb of God who would lay down His life for the sins of the world. This message from John is pointing to the death of the Lord Jesus from the commencement of the gospel.

1.33 'ghost' means 'spirit'.

1.34 'record' means 'testimony' – this is a theme in John's gospel. The testimony of individuals are recorded for us as those who witness to the fact that Jesus is the Christ, the Son of God. Nathanael (1.49); Woman at Sychar's well (4.29); Peter (6.68-69); Blind man (9.38); Martha (11.27); Thomas (20.28)

1.37 'they followed Jesus' – there was someone greater than John the Baptist: Jesus.

1.38 The Lord's first words in John's gospel: 'what seek ye?' – what are you seeking? The most searching question we all must face is what are we looking for in life.

1.41 Andrew's first act as a new disciple was to bring His brother Simon (later called Peter) to Christ. Disciples still bring others to Christ.

1.46 – Nathanael initially doubted His goodness, just as Thomas doubted His resurrection (20.25)

1.47 – 'guile' means 'deceit'

1.48 'I saw thee' – not even 'I knew you'. The Lord Jesus was claiming, as God, to be omnipresent. Although in a real body on earth He still 'saw' Nathanael under the tree because He was there in Spirit.

---

34 And I saw, and bare record that this is the Son of God.

### The Calling of the First Disciples vv.35-51

35 Again the next day after John stood, and two of his disciples;

36 And looking upon Jesus as he walked, he saith, Behold the Lamb of God!

37 And the two disciples heard him speak, and they followed Jesus.

38 Then Jesus turned, and saw them following, and saith unto them, What seek ye? They said unto him, Rabbi, (which is to say, being interpreted, Master,) where dwellest thou?

39 He saith unto them, Come and see. They came and saw where he dwelt, and abode with him that day: for it was about the tenth hour.

40 One of the two which heard John speak, and followed him, was Andrew, Simon Peter's brother.

41 He first findeth his own brother Simon, and saith unto him, We have found the Messias, which is, being interpreted, the Christ.

42 And he brought him to Jesus. And when Jesus beheld him, he said, Thou art Simon the son of Jona: thou shalt be called Cephas, which is by interpretation, A stone.

43 The day following Jesus would go forth into Galilee, and findeth Philip, and saith unto him, Follow me.

44 Now Philip was of Bethsaida, the city of Andrew and Peter.

45 Philip findeth Nathanael, and saith unto him, We have found him, of whom Moses in the law, and the prophets, did write, Jesus of Nazareth, the son of Joseph.

46 And Nathanael said unto him, Can there any good thing come out of Nazareth? Philip saith unto him, Come and see.

47 Jesus saw Nathanael coming to him, and saith of him, Behold an Israelite indeed, in whom is no guile!

48 Nathanael saith unto him, Whence knowest thou me? Jesus answered and said unto him, Before that Philip called thee, when thou wast under the fig tree, I saw thee.

49 Nathanael answered and saith unto him, Rabbi, thou art the Son of God; thou art the King of Israel.
50 Jesus answered and said unto him, Because I said unto thee, I saw thee under the fig tree, believest thou? thou shalt see greater things than these.
51 And he saith unto him, Verily, verily, I say unto you, Hereafter ye shall see heaven open, and the angels of God ascending and descending upon the Son of man.

1.50 'believing is seeing' here and not 'seeing is believing'. By Nathanael believing in the omnipresence of Christ and coming to recognise Him as the eternal Son of God He was entering into a relationship with God which would allow Him to see so much more.
1.51 'Verily Verily' is used 25 times in John's gospel of important sayings. It means 'truly truly';
'The Son of Man' - the Lord is speaking of Himself, it is another title of Christ emphasising His majesty.

A.  What was it that John the Baptist was looking for as he was baptising? v.33.

B.  What are the Lord's first recorded words in John's gospel? v.38.

C.  What was Andrew's first action after receiving Christ? vv.40-42.

D.  What was it that caused Nathanael to believe that Jesus was the Son of God? vv.45-50.

________________________________________

________________________________________

________________________________________

________________________________________

________________________________________

# John 2

## The Establishment of the Son's Authority over Nature and Traditional Religion vv.1-25

### *The First Sign: The Son's Glory in Cana of Galilee vv.1-12*

1 And the third day there was a marriage in Cana of Galilee; and the mother of Jesus was there:

2 And both Jesus was called, and his disciples, to the marriage.

3 And when they wanted wine, the mother of Jesus saith unto him, They have no wine.

4 Jesus saith unto her, Woman, what have I to do with thee? mine hour is not yet come.

5 His mother saith unto the servants, Whatsoever he saith unto you, do it.

6 And there were set there six waterpots of stone, after the manner of the purifying of the Jews, containing two or three firkins apiece.

7 Jesus saith unto them, Fill the waterpots with water. And they filled them up to the brim.

8 And he saith unto them, Draw out now, and bear unto the governor of the feast. And they bare it.

9 When the ruler of the feast had tasted the water that was made wine, and knew not whence it was: (but the servants which drew the water knew;) the governor of the feast called the bridegroom,

10 And saith unto him, Every man at the beginning doth set forth good wine; and when men have well drunk, then that which is worse: but thou hast kept the good wine until now.

11 This beginning of miracles did Jesus in Cana of Galilee, and manifested forth his glory; and his disciples believed on him.

12 After this he went down to Capernaum, he, and his mother, and his brethren, and his disciples: and they continued there not many days.

### *The Son's Temple-Body vv.13-25*

13 And the Jews' passover was at hand, and Jesus went up to Jerusalem.

14 And found in the temple those that sold oxen and sheep and doves, and the changers of money sitting:

15 And when he had made a scourge of small cords,

2.4 'mine hour' – the time to perform His first miracle. The expression 'his hour' generally speaks of His death. A sense of the importance of time and the will of God is a theme in John's gospel as He anticipated His death at Calvary.
(John 7.30, 12.27; 13.1; 17.1).

2.5 What faith is shown by Mary as she had never seen Him do a miracle (see comment on 1.50)!

2.6 'firkins' – a unit of liquid volume containing 9 gallons or about 41 litres.

2.9 'knew not' – this is a theme in John's gospel (e.g. John 1.26; 4.22, 32; 7.28; 9.12; 14.5; 15.21; 20.2, 9, 14; 21.4). The ruler did not know where the wine had come from, only the servants. The Lord Jesus was able to exhibit the most amazing power in the most humble of approaches.

2.11 'beginning' – the Lord Jesus did not perform one miracle until this point at the marriage of Cana when he was around 30 years of age. His miracles were real but few, and all of them were signs to signify who He really was. What the people needed was not more miracles by they needed to believe who He was and place their trust in Him as Saviour.

2.13 'Jews Passover' – this is an interesting expression. Jehovah's Passover (Lev. 23) had become the Jews' Passover. Religion had become so formalised that this special day had become a national cultural event rather than something that honoured God.

2.15 'changers of money' – they had set up stalls so that people could buy sacrifices instead of bringing a sacrifice. Convenience and commercialism entered into God's House, something which was repugnant to the Christ and still is.

2.16 'My father's house' -  the Saviour called Herod's Temple, His Father's House. This was the site of the previous three temples. It had now been turned into a house of merchandise

2.17 "remembered" - this is a theme in John's gospel. Compare 2.17,22; 12.16; 13.7;15.20;16.4.

2.20 Herod's temple commenced being rebuilt in BC19.

2.22 'risen from the dead' - The resurrection of Christ is a key theme in John's gospel and this is the first direct reference to this truth although the subject of life has already been introduced (1.4)

2.25 It was more than seeing miracles that were needed to make people disciples (v23), they had to recognize the sin in their own heart (v25).

he drove them all out of the temple, and the sheep, and the oxen; and poured out the changers' money, and overthrew the tables;

16 And said unto them that sold doves, Take these things hence; make not my Father's house an house of merchandise.

17 And his disciples remembered that it was written, The zeal of thine house hath eaten me up.

18 Then answered the Jews and said unto him, What sign shewest thou unto us, seeing that thou doest these things?

19 Jesus answered and said unto them, Destroy this temple, and in three days I will raise it up.

20 Then said the Jews, Forty and six years was this temple in building, and wilt thou rear it up in three days?

21 But he spake of the temple of his body.

22 When therefore he was risen from the dead, his disciples remembered that he had said this unto them; and they believed the scripture, and the word which Jesus had said.

23 Now when he was in Jerusalem at the passover, in the feast day, many believed in his name, when they saw the miracles which he did.

24 But Jesus did not commit himself unto them, because he knew all men,

25 And needed not that any should testify of man: for he knew what was in man.

A.  Why are Mary's words in verse 5 so amazing?

B.  What was it that grieved the Lord Jesus so much? v.16.

C.  How did the Lord Jesus introduce the truth of the resurrection? vv.19-21.

_______________________________________________

_______________________________________________

_______________________________________________

_______________________________________________

# John 3
## The Establishment of the Son's Authority in Teaching and Testimony vv.1-36
### The Son's Answers to Questions Raised by Nicodemus vv.1-13

1 There was a man of the Pharisees, named Nicodemus, a ruler of the Jews:

2 The same came to Jesus by night, and said unto him, Rabbi, we know that thou art a teacher come from God: for no man can do these miracles that thou doest, except God be with him.

3 **Jesus answered and said unto him, Verily, verily, I say unto thee, Except a man be born again, he cannot see the kingdom of God**.

4 Nicodemus saith unto him, How can a man be born when he is old? can he enter the second time into his mother's womb, and be born?

5 Jesus answered, Verily, verily, I say unto thee, Except a man be born of water and of the Spirit, he cannot enter into the kingdom of God.

6 That which is born of the flesh is flesh; and that which is born of the Spirit is spirit.

7 **Marvel not that I said unto thee, Ye must be born again**.

8 The wind bloweth where it listeth, and thou hearest the sound thereof, but canst not tell whence it cometh, and whither it goeth: so is every one that is born of the Spirit.

9 Nicodemus answered and said unto him, How can these things be?

10 Jesus answered and said unto him, Art thou a master of Israel, and knowest not these things?

11 Verily, verily, I say unto thee, We speak that we do know, and testify that we have seen; and ye receive not our witness.

12 If I have told you earthly things, and ye believe not, how shall ye believe, if I tell you of heavenly things?

13 And no man hath ascended up to heaven, but he that came down from heaven, even the Son of man which is in heaven.

---

3.1 Nicodemus, a religious leader of the strict sect of the Jews (Pharisee), appears three times in John's gospel (3.1-9; 7.50; 19.39). It is here we have the initial dialogue with Christ about spiritual matters. He has certainly become a Christian by chapter 19.

3.2 'Rabbi' – means 'Master'

3.3 'Born again' – or born from above or born of God (see 1.13; 3.7; 1Peter 1.23)

3.7 The Lord is explaining to Nicodemus the most important thing he needed was to be born again. It was not natural birth into our natural family (v4-5) but spiritual birth into the family of God. It was not through human effort but through the Holy Spirit (verse 6) on the basis of simple faith in Christ.

3.8 'wind bloweth where it listeth' – means 'the winds blows where it pleases'
Just as you cannot explain or predict the movement of the wind neither can you explain God's salvation.

***The Son as the Revealer of Eternal Life vv.14-21***

14 And as Moses lifted up the serpent in the wilderness, even so must the Son of man be lifted up:

15 That whosoever believeth in him should not perish, but have eternal life.

16 **For God so loved the world, that he gave his only begotten Son, that whosoever believeth in him should not perish, but have everlasting life**.

17 For God sent not his Son into the world to condemn the world; but that the world through him might be saved.

18 He that believeth on him is not condemned: but he that believeth not is condemned already, because he hath not believed in the name of the only begotten Son of God.

19 And this is the condemnation, that light is come into the world, and men loved darkness rather than light, because their deeds were evil.

20 For every one that doeth evil hateth the light, neither cometh to the light, lest his deeds should be reproved.

21 But he that doeth truth cometh to the light, that his deeds may be made manifest, that they are wrought in God.

***John the Baptist's Last Testimony Concerning the Son vv.22-36***

22 After these things came Jesus and his disciples into the land of Judaea; and there he tarried with them, and baptized.

23 And John also was baptizing in Aenon near to Salim, because there was much water there: and they came, and were baptized.

24 For John was not yet cast into prison.

25 Then there arose a question between some of John's disciples and the Jews about purifying.

26 And they came unto John, and said unto him, Rabbi, he that was with thee beyond Jordan, to whom thou barest witness, behold, the same baptizeth, and all men come to him.

27 John answered and said, A man can receive nothing, except it be given him from heaven.

28 Ye yourselves bear me witness, that I said, I am not the Christ, but that I am sent before him.

---

3.14 'Son of Man' – a title of the Lord Jesus as the Messiah. It stresses His Majesty and the dignity which he conferred upon Man (see 1.51)

3.14 – this is a reference to Numbers 21.8 where the children of Israel who had been bitten by snakes could look at a brass snake on a pole and be healed. So the Lord Jesus would be lifted up upon a cross and provide healing to all who were afflicted by their sins. He defeated the devil (serpent) at the Cross.

3.16 – See article on first page

3.17 'saved' – An important Bible word. The word saved means to be rescued from our sins, a wasted life, and hell (John 5.34; 10.9; Acts 4.12).

3.20 'reproved' means 'refuted', 'disapproved'.

3.21 – Truth can tried, tested and illuminated but it will always be truth. Error is always exposed in the light.

3.23 'much water' - a lot of water is required for baptism. John's baptism required the repentance of sin and immersion under water.

3.29 John took the position, along with all the Old Testament believers of being the "friend of the bridegroom". The bridegroom is Christ. The church is the bride (Eph. 5.23)

3.31 John constantly acknowledged that the Lord Jesus, as God, came from heaven.

3.33 'set to his seal' means 'has certified'.

3.35 The relationship within the Trinity is one of love (John 5.20; 10.17; 14.31).

3.36 The simplicity of the Gospel Message. To have the Lord Jesus Christ as Saviour is to have everything – everlasting life. To refuse Him is to know eternal loss and punishment.

29 He that hath the bride is the bridegroom: but the friend of the bridegroom, which standeth and heareth him, rejoiceth greatly because of the bridegroom's voice: this my joy therefore is fulfilled.

30 He must increase, but I must decrease.

31 He that cometh from above is above all: he that is of the earth is earthly, and speaketh of the earth: he that cometh from heaven is above all.

32 And what he hath seen and heard, that he testifieth; and no man receiveth his testimony.

33 He that hath received his testimony hath set to his seal that God is true.

34 For he whom God hath sent speaketh the words of God: for God giveth not the Spirit by measure unto him.

35 The Father loveth the Son, and hath given all things into his hand.

36 He that believeth on the Son hath everlasting life: and he that believeth not the Son shall not see life; but the wrath of God abideth on him.

# *Reflective Questions and Notes*

A.  Why must everyone be born again? v.3.


B.  What is God's gift to those who believe in His Only Begotten Son? v.16.


C.  What is the position of those who 'believe not' - see v.18, 36?


D.  What position did John take in relation to the Christ? v.29.

______________________________________

______________________________________

______________________________________

______________________________________

______________________________________

# John 4

## The Establishment by the Son of True Worship vv.1-54

### *True Water vv.1-18*

1 When therefore the Lord knew how the Pharisees had heard that Jesus made and baptized more disciples than John,

2 (Though Jesus himself baptized not, but his disciples,)

3 He left Judaea, and departed again into Galilee.

4 And he must needs go through Samaria.

5 Then cometh he to a city of Samaria, which is called Sychar, near to the parcel of ground that Jacob gave to his son Joseph.

6 Now Jacob's well was there. Jesus therefore, being wearied with his journey, sat thus on the well: and it was about the sixth hour.

7 There cometh a woman of Samaria to draw water: Jesus saith unto her, Give me to drink.

8 (For his disciples were gone away unto the city to buy meat.)

9 Then saith the woman of Samaria unto him, How is it that thou, being a Jew, askest drink of me, which am a woman of Samaria? for the Jews have no dealings with the Samaritans.

10 Jesus answered and said unto her, If thou knewest the gift of God, and who it is that saith to thee, Give me to drink; thou wouldest have asked of him, and he would have given thee living water.

11 The woman saith unto him, Sir, thou hast nothing to draw with, and the well is deep: from whence then hast thou that living water?

12 Art thou greater than our father Jacob, which gave us the well, and drank thereof himself, and his children, and his cattle?

13 Jesus answered and said unto her, Whosoever drinketh of this water shall thirst again:

14 But whosoever drinketh of the water that I shall give him shall never thirst; but the water that I shall give him shall be in him a well of water springing up into everlasting life.

---

4.2 The Lord showed tremendous wisdom allowing his disciples to do the baptisms – just in case anyone thought they were a superior Christian as they had been baptized by the Lord. It was the work of Christ at the cross and His resurrection that saved people and not the Baptiser.

4.5 This is a reference to Genesis 48.12-22.

4.7 The Lord's first saying at the well is one of grace as He asks for a drink. This is the One who made the Oceans and could turn water into wine.

4.9 Initially the Lord received a hostile response based on ethnicity and gender.

4.10 The Lord responds a second time in kindness claiming that He can provide living water.

4.11 The lady responsed by saying that the Lord Jesus does not have the capacity to meet her need (many have thought this since) having neither a bucket nor the means to drop the bucket in the well.

4.13 The Lord responds a third time saying that her needs were not merely physical (she had thirsts that were far deeper than this) and that He could meet her spiritual needs in full by providing her with everlasting life – the life of God.

15 The woman saith unto him, Sir, give me this water, that I thirst not, neither come hither to draw.

16 Jesus saith unto her, Go, call thy husband, and come hither.

17 The woman answered and said, I have no husband. Jesus said unto her, Thou hast well said, I have no husband:

18 For thou hast had five husbands; and he whom thou now hast is not thy husband: in that saidst thou truly.

### True Worship vv.19-26

19 The woman saith unto him, Sir, I perceive that thou art a prophet.

20 Our fathers worshipped in this mountain; and ye say, that in Jerusalem is the place where men ought to worship.

21 Jesus saith unto her, Woman, believe me, the hour cometh, when ye shall neither in this mountain, nor yet at Jerusalem, worship the Father.

22 Ye worship ye know not what: we know what we worship: for salvation is of the Jews.

23 But the hour cometh, and now is, when the true worshippers shall worship the Father in spirit and in truth: for the Father seeketh such to worship him.

24 God is a Spirit: and they that worship him must worship him in spirit and in truth.

25 The woman saith unto him, I know that Messias cometh, which is called Christ: when he is come, he will tell us all things.

26 Jesus saith unto her, I that speak unto thee am he.

### True Witness vv.27-42

27 And upon this came his disciples, and marvelled that he talked with the woman: yet no man said, What seekest thou? or, Why talkest thou with her?

28 The woman then left her waterpot, and went her way into the city, and saith to the men,

29 **Come, see a man, which told me all things that ever I did: is not this the Christ?**

30 Then they went out of the city, and came unto him.

31 In the mean while his disciples prayed him, saying, Master, eat.

4.18 The lady was interested and wanted salvation but had to understand that repentance of sin was necessary to receive everlasting life. The Lord spoke a fourth time, putting His finger right on the problem in her life.

4.19-20 The lady understood that the Lord Jesus was all knowing and knew everything about her. She wanted to know how God could accept her as a worshipper with all her sin. She was enquiring whether external religion was what she required.

4. 21-23 The Lord responded by telling her that what she required was not religion in a particular place but a work of the Holy Spirit in her heart. It was not external religious form that she needed but an inward relationship with God. She could be a worshipper of God.

4.25 The lady longs for the Messiah to come to explain it all to her.

4.26 The Lord Jesus speaks for the seventh time and claims to be the Messiah.

4.28-29 The lady receives salvation. She left her water pot behind - even legitimate things seemed irrelevant - and ran into the city with joy to tell others about the Saviour.

4.34  The will of the Father is a theme in John's gospel (5.30; 6.36, 38, 39; 7.17; 17.4). The Lord Jesus was the only one who fulfilled the Father's will in its entirety and ultimately went to the cross to fulfil His will.

4.35 When men saw a bare desert, the Saviour saw a field ready to be harvested. Today people are still seeking after peace, hope and salvation from God. Some would see one woman at a well, he saw a whole city who would be saved through the testimony of one woman.

4.39 A reminder to us that God often uses the simple testimony of a Christian to bring others to salvation

4.44 'a prophet has no honour in his own country' - an idiomatic phrase that means that often times leaders are not appreciated by their own people.

32 But he said unto them, I have meat to eat that ye know not of.

33 Therefore said the disciples one to another, Hath any man brought him ought to eat?

34 Jesus saith unto them, My meat is to do the will of him that sent me, and to finish his work.

35 Say not ye, There are yet four months, and then cometh harvest? behold, I say unto you, Lift up your eyes, and look on the fields; for they are white already to harvest.

36 And he that reapeth receiveth wages, and gathereth fruit unto life eternal: that both he that soweth and he that reapeth may rejoice together.

37 And herein is that saying true, One soweth, and another reapeth.

38 I sent you to reap that whereon ye bestowed no labour: other men laboured, and ye are entered into their labours.

39 And many of the Samaritans of that city believed on him for the saying of the woman, which testified, He told me all that ever I did.

40 So when the Samaritans were come unto him, they besought him that he would tarry with them: and he abode there two days.

41 And many more believed because of his own word;

42 And said unto the woman, Now we believe, not because of thy saying: for we have heard him ourselves, and know that this is indeed the Christ, the Saviour of the world.

### The Second Sign: Faith in the Lord's Word vv.43-54

43 Now after two days he departed thence, and went into Galilee.

44 For Jesus himself testified, that a prophet hath no honour in his own country.

45 Then when he was come into Galilee, the Galilaeans received him, having seen all the things that he did at Jerusalem at the feast: for they also went unto the feast.

### The Nobleman's Son Receives Life

46 So Jesus came again into Cana of Galilee, where he made the water wine. And there was a certain nobleman, whose son was sick at Capernaum.

47 When he heard that Jesus was come out of Judaea into Galilee, he went unto him, and besought him that he would come down, and heal his son: for he was at the point of death.

48 Then said Jesus unto him, Except ye see signs and wonders, ye will not believe.

49 The nobleman saith unto him, Sir, come down ere my child die.

50 Jesus saith unto him, Go thy way; thy son liveth. And the man believed the word that Jesus had spoken unto him, and he went his way.

51 And as he was now going down, his servants met him, and told him, saying, Thy son liveth.

52 Then enquired he of them the hour when he began to amend. And they said unto him, Yesterday at the seventh hour the fever left him.

53 So the father knew that it was at the same hour, in the which Jesus said unto him, Thy son liveth: and himself believed, and his whole house.

54 This is again the second miracle that Jesus did, when he was come out of Judaea into Galilee.

The Nobleman believes three times (v47,50,53).

V47 – He Believed that Jesus was the **way** to blessing.

V50 - He Believed the Lord Jesus was the **truth.**

**V53 -** He Believed that the Lord Jesus was the **life (John 14.6).**

V54 – This miracle was done at a distance. The power lay in the word of Christ and not in His touch.

# *Reflective Questions and Notes*

A.  What does the woman initially call the Lord? v.9.
How does she finally address the Lord? v.29.

B.  What did the Lord promise He would give the woman if she believed? vv.10,14.

C.  What was the One thing that spoke to the woman more than anything else? v.29.

D.  At what hour was the Nobleman's Son healed? Why is this important to the Nobleman? vv.52-53.

__________________________________

__________________________________

__________________________________

__________________________________

__________________________________

# John 5

## The Son of God Rejected vv.1-47

### *The Third Sign: Healing on the Sabbath Day vv.1-15*

1 After this there was a feast of the Jews; and Jesus went up to Jerusalem.

2 Now there is at Jerusalem by the sheep market a pool, which is called in the Hebrew tongue Bethesda, having five porches.

3 In these lay a great multitude of impotent folk, of blind, halt, withered, waiting for the moving of the water.

4 For an angel went down at a certain season into the pool, and troubled the water: whosoever then first after the troubling of the water stepped in was made whole of whatsoever disease he had.

5 And a certain man was there, which had an infirmity thirty and eight years.

6 When Jesus saw him lie, and knew that he had been now a long time in that case, he saith unto him, Wilt thou be made whole?

7 The impotent man answered him, Sir, I have no man, when the water is troubled, to put me into the pool: but while I am coming, another steppeth down before me.

8 Jesus saith unto him, Rise, take up thy bed, and walk.

9 And immediately the man was made whole, and took up his bed, and walked: and on the same day was the sabbath.

10 The Jews therefore said unto him that was cured, It is the sabbath day: it is not lawful for thee to carry thy bed.

11 He answered them, He that made me whole, the same said unto me, Take up thy bed, and walk.

12 Then asked they him, What man is that which said unto thee, Take up thy bed, and walk?

13 And he that was healed wist not who it was: for Jesus had conveyed himself away, a multitude being in that place.

14 Afterward Jesus findeth him in the temple, and said unto him, Behold, thou art made whole: sin no more, lest a worse thing come unto thee.

15 The man departed, and told the Jews that it was Jesus, which had made him whole.

### *The Father and the Son vv.16-30*

16 And therefore did the Jews persecute Jesus, and sought to slay him, because he had done these things on the sabbath day.

17 But Jesus answered them, My Father worketh hitherto, and I work.

**The Paralysed Man by the Pool of Bethesda finds wholeness**

5.3 'halt' means 'crippled'; 'withered' means 'paralysed'.

5.4 There was a belief amongst those who lay by the pool that the stirrings of the water came from a supernatural source. People today who have significant physical needs can sometimes be attracted to mystical methods of healing.

5.5 'infirmity' means 'invalid'.

5.7 'impotent' means 'weak', 'powerless', 'invalid'.

5.13 'wist' means 'knew'.

5.16 These Jews would prefer to see the man paralysed than break one of their man-made rules about healing on the Sabbath day. Religion can blind.

**The Lord Jesus Speaks of the Father (just before 5.18)**

5.18 – The Jews understood that a claim to be the Son of God was a claim to be on equality with God.

5.19 If the Son could do something by Himself there would be two Gods. But there is only one God. We cannot divide the Father from the Son.
'Likewise' – not only does He do exactly the same things as the Father but He does them in exactly the same way as the Father - with the same motive, method and manner.

5.21 The Son of God raises the dead.
5.22 The Son of God is the judge of all things.
5.23 Equal honour must be given to the Son as is given to the Father. To dishonour the Son is to dishonour the Father.

5.31 He is not saying that His testimony is untrustworthy! He is God! He is saying if He was the only One who bore testimony to Him being able to give everlasting life then it would not be true. He will now list other witnesses.

5.32 – the testimony of the Holy Spirit.
5.33 – the testimony of John the Baptist.

18 Therefore the Jews sought the more to kill him, because he not only had broken the sabbath, but said also that God was his Father, making himself equal with God.
19 Then answered Jesus and said unto them, Verily, verily, I say unto you, The Son can do nothing of himself, but what he seeth the Father do: for what things soever he doeth, these also doeth the Son likewise.
20 For the Father loveth the Son, and sheweth him all things that himself doeth: and he will shew him greater works than these, that ye may marvel.
21 For as the Father raiseth up the dead, and quickeneth them; even so the Son quickeneth whom he will.
22 For the Father judgeth no man, but hath committed all judgment unto the Son:
23 That all men should honour the Son, even as they honour the Father. He that honoureth not the Son honoureth not the Father which hath sent him.
24 **Verily, verily, I say unto you, He that heareth my word, and believeth on him that sent me, hath everlasting life, and shall not come into condemnation; but is passed from death unto life**.
25 Verily, verily, I say unto you, The hour is coming, and now is, when the dead shall hear the voice of the Son of God: and they that hear shall live.
26 For as the Father hath life in himself; so hath he given to the Son to have life in himself;
27 And hath given him authority to execute judgment also, because he is the Son of man.
28 Marvel not at this: for the hour is coming, in the which all that are in the graves shall hear his voice,
29 And shall come forth; they that have done good, unto the resurrection of life; and they that have done evil, unto the resurrection of damnation.
30 I can of mine own self do nothing: as I hear, I judge: and my judgment is just; because I seek not mine own will, but the will of the Father which hath sent me.

### Witness to the Son vv.31-47

31 If I bear witness of myself, my witness is not true.
32 There is another that beareth witness of me; and I know that the witness which he witnesseth of me is true.
33 Ye sent unto John, and he bare witness unto the truth.
34 But I receive not testimony from man: but these things I say, that ye might be saved.
35 He was a burning and a shining light: and ye were willing for a season to rejoice in his light.

36 But I have greater witness than that of John: for the works which the Father hath given me to finish, the same works that I do, bear witness of me, that the Father hath sent me.

37 And the Father himself, which hath sent me, hath borne witness of me. Ye have neither heard his voice at any time, nor seen his shape.

38 And ye have not his word abiding in you: for whom he hath sent, him ye believe not.

39 Search the scriptures; for in them ye think ye have eternal life: and they are they which testify of me.

40 **And ye will not come to me, that ye might have life**.

41 I receive not honour from men.

42 But I know you, that ye have not the love of God in you.

43 I am come in my Father's name, and ye receive me not: if another shall come in his own name, him ye will receive.

44 How can ye believe, which receive honour one of another, and seek not the honour that cometh from God only?

45 Do not think that I will accuse you to the Father: there is one that accuseth you, even Moses, in whom ye trust.

46 For had ye believed Moses, ye would have believed me; for he wrote of me.

47 But if ye believe not his writings, how shall ye believe my words?

5.36 – the testimony of the works of the Father.

5.39 – the testimony of Holy Scripture.

5.45–47 the testimony of Moses.

A.  What did the Jews understand Him to mean when the Lord Jesus said God was His Father? v.18.

B.  What is the promise to those who hear His word and believe on Him as Saviour? v.24.

C.  What witnesses does He list to support His claims? vv.31-39.

_______________________________________

_______________________________________

_______________________________________

_______________________________________

# John 6
## The Bread of Life Rejected vv.1-71
### The Fourth Sign: The Feeding of the Five Thousand vv.1-14

1 After these things Jesus went over the sea of Galilee, which is the sea of Tiberias.

2 And a great multitude followed him, because they saw his miracles which he did on them that were diseased.

3 And Jesus went up into a mountain, and there he sat with his disciples.

4 And the passover, a feast of the Jews, was nigh.

5 When Jesus then lifted up his eyes, and saw a great company come unto him, he saith unto Philip, Whence shall we buy bread, that these may eat?

6 And this he said to prove him: for he himself knew what he would do.

7 Philip answered him, Two hundred pennyworth of bread is not sufficient for them, that every one of them may take a little.

8 One of his disciples, Andrew, Simon Peter's brother, saith unto him,

9 There is a lad here, which hath five barley loaves, and two small fishes: but what are they among so many?

10 And Jesus said, Make the men sit down. Now there was much grass in the place. So the men sat down, in number about five thousand.

11 And Jesus took the loaves; and when he had given thanks, he distributed to the disciples, and the disciples to them that were set down; and likewise of the fishes as much as they would.

12 When they were filled, he said unto his disciples, Gather up the fragments that remain, that nothing be lost.

13 Therefore they gathered them together, and filled twelve baskets with the fragments of the five barley loaves, which remained over and above unto them that had eaten.

14 Then those men, when they had seen the miracle that Jesus did, said, This is of a truth that prophet that should come into the world.

### The Fifth Sign: The Lord Walking on the Sea vv.15-24

15 When Jesus therefore perceived that they would come and take him by force, to make him a king, he departed again into a mountain himself alone.

16 And when even was now come, his disciples went down unto the sea,

**The Lord Jesus by the Sea of Galilee – the bread of life**

6.1 'Sea of Tiberias' – the Roman name for the Sea of Galilee.

6.2 'sat' – see references for the Lord seated in John 4.6; 6.3; 8.2; 12.2; 12.14; 13.12; 19.13.

6.4 The Passover feasts which take place on the 14th day of the first Jewish month, (Nisan 14 – around March/April) punctuate John's Gospel and gives the years of the Lord's public teaching (see John 2.13,23; 6.4; 11.55; 12.1; 13.1; 18.28,39; 19.14).

6.7 One penny was a labouring man's wages for a day (Matthew 20.2). 200 pennies would be a lot of money - almost a year's wages.

6.10 This miracle is the only miracle recorded in all four gospels.

6.11 Even the Creator gave thanks for food.

6.19 30 furlongs is around 3.75 miles.

17 And entered into a ship, and went over the sea toward Capernaum. And it was now dark, and Jesus was not come to them.

18 And the sea arose by reason of a great wind that blew.

19 So when they had rowed about five and twenty or thirty furlongs, they see Jesus walking on the sea, and drawing nigh unto the ship: and they were afraid.

20 But he saith unto them, It is I; be not afraid.

21 Then they willingly received him into the ship: and immediately the ship was at the land whither they went.

22 The day following, when the people which stood on the other side of the sea saw that there was none other boat there, save that one whereinto his disciples were entered, and that Jesus went not with his disciples into the boat, but that his disciples were gone away alone;

23 (Howbeit there came other boats from Tiberias nigh unto the place where they did eat bread, after that the Lord had given thanks:)

24 When the people therefore saw that Jesus was not there, neither his disciples, they also took shipping, and came to Capernaum, seeking for Jesus.

### The First Question: vv.25-27

6.25 'Rabbi' means 'Master'; 'hither' means 'here'.

25 And when they had found him on the other side of the sea, they said unto him, Rabbi, when camest thou hither?

6.26-27 The Lord Jesus warns that people's immediate needs (e.g. food) can sometimes stifle their hunger for eternal and spiritual needs. He invites us to go in for the bigger issue – eternal life.

26 Jesus answered them and said, Verily, verily, I say unto you, Ye seek me, not because ye saw the miracles, but because ye did eat of the loaves, and were filled.

27 Labour not for the meat which perisheth, but for that meat which endureth unto everlasting life, which the Son of man shall give unto you: for him hath God the Father sealed.

### The Second Question: vv.28-29

6.28-29 – The Lord explains that it is not 'good works' that saves us, but believing on Christ (Ephesians 2.8).

28 Then said they unto him, What shall we do, that we might work the works of God?

29 Jesus answered and said unto them, This is the work of God, that ye believe on him whom he hath sent.

### The Third Question: vv.30-33

30 They said therefore unto him, What sign shewest thou then, that we may see, and believe thee? what dost thou work?

6.31 Reference to Exodus 16 where Israel ate Manna for 40 years in the wilderness.
6.32 True Light (1.9); True Bread (6.32), True Vine (15.1); True God (17.3).

31 Our fathers did eat manna in the desert; as it is written, He gave them bread from heaven to eat.

32 Then Jesus said unto them, Verily, verily, I say unto you, Moses gave you not that bread from heaven; but my Father giveth you the true bread from heaven.

33 For the bread of God is he which cometh down from heaven, and giveth life unto the world.

### The Fourth Question: vv.34-40

34 Then said they unto him, Lord, evermore give us this bread.

35 **And Jesus said unto them, I am the bread of life: he that cometh to me shall never hunger; and he that believeth on me shall never thirst**.

36 But I said unto you, That ye also have seen me, and believe not.

37 All that the Father giveth me shall come to me; and him that cometh to me I will in no wise cast out.

38 For I came down from heaven, not to do mine own will, but the will of him that sent me.

39 And this is the Father's will which hath sent me, that of all which he hath given me I should lose nothing, but should raise it up again at the last day.

40 And this is the will of him that sent me, that every one which seeth the Son, and believeth on him, may have everlasting life: and I will raise him up at the last day.

### The Fifth Question: vv.41-51

41 The Jews then murmured at him, because he said, I am the bread which came down from heaven.

42 And they said, Is not this Jesus, the son of Joseph, whose father and mother we know? how is it then that he saith, I came down from heaven?

43 Jesus therefore answered and said unto them, Murmur not among yourselves.

44 No man can come to me, except the Father which hath sent me draw him: and I will raise him up at the last day.

45 It is written in the prophets, And they shall be all taught of God. Every man therefore that hath heard, and hath learned of the Father, cometh unto me.

46 Not that any man hath seen the Father, save he which is of God, he hath seen the Father.

47 Verily, verily, I say unto you, He that believeth on me hath everlasting life.

48 I am that bread of life.

49 Your fathers did eat manna in the wilderness, and are dead.

50 This is the bread which cometh down from heaven, that a man may eat thereof, and not die.

51 I am the living bread which came down from heaven: if any man eat of this bread, he shall live for ever: and the bread that I will give is my flesh, which I will give for the life of the world.

6.35 Provision for all: Our deepest hungers can be fully met in Christ

6.37 All who come for salvation will be received. No one will be turned away.

6.39 The Salvation of Christ is eternal. You cannot be saved and then lost.

6.51 Our salvation is entirely dependent on Him laying down His life for us

6.53-57 The Lord is not talking literally but He uses powerful language to show us that our salvation allows us to enjoy intimate fellowship and communion with Him. It is not merely a theoretical knowledge of Him but a living, practical relationship.

6.60-64 Not all are prepared to accept Christ as Saviour and sadly remain unbelievers.

6.68 Testimony that Jesus is the Son of God, on the basis of His words.

6.70 - 'devil' means 'demon'. There is only one devil but many demons.

### The Sixth Question: vv.52-59

52 The Jews therefore strove among themselves, saying, How can this man give us his flesh to eat?

53 Then Jesus said unto them, Verily, verily, I say unto you, Except ye eat the flesh of the Son of man, and drink his blood, ye have no life in you.

54 Whoso eateth my flesh, and drinketh my blood, hath eternal life; and I will raise him up at the last day.

55 For my flesh is meat indeed, and my blood is drink indeed.

56 He that eateth my flesh, and drinketh my blood, dwelleth in me, and I in him.

57 As the living Father hath sent me, and I live by the Father: so he that eateth me, even he shall live by me.

58 This is that bread which came down from heaven: not as your fathers did eat manna, and are dead: he that eateth of this bread shall live for ever.

59 These things said he in the synagogue, as he taught in Capernaum.

### The Seventh Question: vv.60-67

60 Many therefore of his disciples, when they had heard this, said, This is an hard saying; who can hear it?

61 When Jesus knew in himself that his disciples murmured at it, he said unto them, Doth this offend you?

62 What and if ye shall see the Son of man ascend up where he was before?

63 It is the spirit that quickeneth; the flesh profiteth nothing: the words that I speak unto you, they are spirit, and they are life.

64 But there are some of you that believe not. For Jesus knew from the beginning who they were that believed not, and who should betray him.

65 And he said, Therefore said I unto you, that no man can come unto me, except it were given unto him of my Father.

66 From that time many of his disciples went back, and walked no more with him.

67 Then said Jesus unto the twelve, Will ye also go away?

### The Eighth Question: vv.68-71

68 **Then Simon Peter answered him, Lord, to whom shall we go? thou hast the words of eternal life**.

69 **And we believe and are sure that thou art that Christ, the Son of the living God**.

70 Jesus answered them, Have not I chosen you twelve, and one of you is a devil?

71 He spake of Judas Iscariot the son of Simon: for he it was that should betray him, being one of the twelve.

A.  What are the two sign miracles the Lord performed in this chapter?

B.  What is the work of God? vv.28-29.

C.  What do you think the Lord meant in verse 35?

D.  What was the Lord referring to in verse 51 when He said, "The bread that I will give is my flesh"?

__________________________________

__________________________________

__________________________________

__________________________________

__________________________________

# John 7

## The Christ Rejected vv.1-53
### *Before the Feast of Tabernacles vv.1-10*

1 After these things Jesus walked in Galilee: for he would not walk in Jewry, because the Jews sought to kill him.
2 Now the Jew's feast of tabernacles was at hand.
3 His brethren therefore said unto him, Depart hence, and go into Judaea, that thy disciples also may see the works that thou doest.
4 For there is no man that doeth any thing in secret, and he himself seeketh to be known openly. If thou do these things, shew thyself to the world.
5 For neither did his brethren believe in him.
6 Then Jesus said unto them, My time is not yet come: but your time is alway ready.
7 The world cannot hate you; but me it hateth, because I testify of it, that the works thereof are evil.
8 Go ye up unto this feast: I go not up yet unto this feast: for my time is not yet full come.
9 When he had said these words unto them, he abode still in Galilee.
10 But when his brethren were gone up, then went he also up unto the feast, not openly, but as it were in secret.

### *During the Feast of Tabernacles vv.11-36*

11 Then the Jews sought him at the feast, and said, Where is he?
12 And there was much murmuring among the people concerning him: for some said, He is a good man: others said, Nay; but he deceiveth the people.
13 Howbeit no man spake openly of him for fear of the Jews.
14 Now about the midst of the feast Jesus went up into the temple, and taught.
15 And the Jews marvelled, saying, How knoweth this man letters, having never learned?
16 Jesus answered them, and said, My doctrine is not mine, but his that sent me.
17 If any man will do his will, he shall know of the doctrine, whether it be of God, or whether I speak of myself.
18 He that speaketh of himself seeketh his own glory: but he that seeketh his glory that sent him, the same is true, and no unrighteousness is in him.
19 Did not Moses give you the law, and yet none of you keepeth the law? Why go ye about to kill me?
20 The people answered and said, Thou hast a devil: who goeth about to kill thee?

---

7.1 Jewry is a name for Judea – an area around Jerusalem and south of Jerusalem towards Egypt.

7.2 The Feast of Tabernacles is the last of the feast days in September/October time (Leviticus 23).

7.4 This is the attitude of the world – if you've got it flaunt it. The Lord had a different way.

7.6-8 The Lord's sense of timing is theme in the gospel of John (1.18; 4.23; 5.6, 37; 6.666; 11.39; 14.9; 16.2,4,25; 21.14).

7.15 'letters' – they were effectively saying how can He read as He is not educated. What a paradox - He was the Word (1.1); the originator and totality of all knowledge.

7.18 This is a statement of the impeccability of Christ.

7.20 The people seem unaware of the plot outlined in 7.1 and therefore only a few knew (see 7.25).

21 Jesus answered and said unto them, I have done one work, and ye all marvel.

22 Moses therefore gave unto you circumcision; (not because it is of Moses, but of the fathers;) and ye on the sabbath day circumcise a man.

23 If a man on the sabbath day receive circumcision, that the law of Moses should not be broken; are ye angry at me, because I have made a man every whit whole on the sabbath day?

24 Judge not according to the appearance, but judge righteous judgment.

25 Then said some of them of Jerusalem, Is not this he, whom they seek to kill?

26 But, lo, he speaketh boldly, and they say nothing unto him. Do the rulers know indeed that this is the very Christ?

27 Howbeit we know this man whence he is: but when Christ cometh, no man knoweth whence he is.

28 Then cried Jesus in the temple as he taught, saying, Ye both know me, and ye know whence I am: and I am not come of myself, but he that sent me is true, whom ye know not.

29 But I know him: for I am from him, and he hath sent me.

30 Then they sought to take him: but no man laid hands on him, because his hour was not yet come.

31 And many of the people believed on him, and said, When Christ cometh, will he do more miracles than these which this man hath done?

32 The Pharisees heard that the people murmured such things concerning him; and the Pharisees and the chief priests sent officers to take him.

33 Then said Jesus unto them, Yet a little while am I with you, and then I go unto him that sent me.

34 Ye shall seek me, and shall not find me: and where I am, thither ye cannot come.

35 Then said the Jews among themselves, Whither will he go, that we shall not find him? will he go unto the dispersed among the Gentiles, and teach the Gentiles?

36 What manner of saying is this that he said, Ye shall seek me, and shall not find me: and where I am, thither ye cannot come?

***At the End of the Feast of Tabernacles vv.37-39***

37 **In the last day, that great day of the feast, Jesus stood and cried, saying, If any man thirst, let him come unto me, and drink**.

38 He that believeth on me, as the scripture hath said, out of his belly shall flow rivers of living water.

---

7.22-24 'circumcision' – a Jewish surgical procedure on male babies at 8 days old where the foreskin is cut off and is seen as a cultural mark of the nation.

7.29 What a claim!

7.33-37 The Lord is referring to the fact that He is going back to heaven.

7.37 The feast ritual involved priests carrying water into the temple as a reminder of the water in the wilderness that spouted out from the rock (Exodus 17.6). The paradox is that the water from the rock spoke of Christ (1Cor.10.1-3) and the ritual was being done in front of Him without them knowing Who He was – the water of life.

7.39 The Spirit of God is a divine person, and is given to all who believe in Christ (John 14.17; Ephesians 1.13).
'Glorified' – speaking of the ascension of Christ back to the Father when He would send the Holy Spirit (16.7).

7.42 The Lord Jesus was born in Bethlehem as the scriptures foretold over 700 years before He was born (Micah 5.2).

7.46 This is an incredible statement from his enemies.

7.50 'Nicodemus' - see 3.1-14.

7.52 'Galilee?' The prophet Jonah came from Galilee and there were others. Clever people can sometimes be wrong even when they make proud and bold pronouncements.

39 (But this spake he of the Spirit, which they that believe on him should receive: for the Holy Ghost was not yet given; because that Jesus was not yet glorified.)

### After the Feast of Tabernacles vv.40-53

40 Many of the people therefore, when they heard this saying, said, Of a truth this is the Prophet.

41 Others said, This is the Christ. But some said, Shall Christ come out of Galilee?

42 Hath not the scripture said, That Christ cometh of the seed of David, and out of the town of Bethlehem, where David was?

43 So there was a division among the people because of him.

44 And some of them would have taken him; but no man laid hands on him.

45 Then came the officers to the chief priests and Pharisees; and they said unto them, Why have ye not brought him?

46 The officers answered, Never man spake like this man.

47 Then answered them the Pharisees, Are ye also deceived?

48 Have any of the rulers or of the Pharisees believed on him?

49 But this people who knoweth not the law are cursed.

50 Nicodemus saith unto them, (he that came to Jesus by night, being one of them,)

51 Doth our law judge any man, before it hear him, and know what he doeth?

52 They answered and said unto him, Art thou also of Galilee? Search, and look: for out of Galilee ariseth no prophet.

53 And every man went unto his own house.

# Reflective Questions and Notes

A.  Why is the question posed by the Jews in verse 15 a paradox?

B.  Why were the Jews being hypocritical in vv.22-24?

C.  What does living water speak of? vv.37-39.

D.  What did the officers of the temple say about Christ? v.46.

_______________________________________________

_______________________________________________

_______________________________________________

_______________________________________________

# John 8
## The I Am" Rejected vv.1-59
### *The Woman not Condemned vv.1-11*

8.1 – see 7.53. The One who was the Creator of the Universe (1.1) and He had nowhere to call home (1.10).

8.8 'convicted by their own conscience'- there is an inbuilt regulator in every life which tells us whether we are doing right or wrong (Romans 2.15).

8.9 -'beginning at the eldest unto the last'– the oldest felt their own hypocrisy and sin the most and so they left first but they all had to leave eventually as 'all have sinned' (Rom. 3.23).
'Jesus was left alone' – He is the only One that was 'without sin' (v7) and therefore able to make a righteous assessment (judgment).

8.11 'Neither do I condemn...... Go and sin no more' . Having received salvation the Lord expects us to live a changed life.

8.12 See also 9.5; 12.46

8.14 'whence' means 'from where'; 'whither' means 'to where'

8.15 'I judge no man'- in context this means 'I judge no one by a natural (fleshly) standard' (as in 8.1-11) but, as verses 16-18 bear

1 Jesus went unto the mount of Olives.

2 And early in the morning he came again into the temple, and all the people came unto him; and he sat down, and taught them.

3 And the scribes and Pharisees brought unto him a woman taken in adultery; and when they had set her in the midst,

4 They say unto him, Master, this woman was taken in adultery, in the very act.

5 Now Moses in the law commanded us, that such should be stoned: but what sayest thou?

6 This they said, tempting him, that they might have to accuse him. But Jesus stooped down, and with his finger wrote on the ground, as though he heard them not.

7 So when they continued asking him, he lifted up himself, and said unto them, He that is without sin among you, let him first cast a stone at her.

8 And again he stooped down, and wrote on the ground.

9 And they which heard it, being convicted by their own conscience, went out one by one, beginning at the eldest, even unto the last: and Jesus was left alone, and the woman standing in the midst.

10 When Jesus had lifted up himself, and saw none but the woman, he said unto her, Woman, where are those thine accusers? hath no man condemned thee?

11 She said, No man, Lord. And Jesus said unto her, Neither do I condemn thee: go, and sin no more.

### *Double Testimony vv.12-20*

12 **Then spake Jesus again unto them, saying, I am the light of the world: he that followeth me shall not walk in darkness, but shall have the light of life**.

13 The Pharisees therefore said unto him, Thou bearest record of thyself; thy record is not true.

14 Jesus answered and said unto them, Though I bear record of myself, yet my record is true: for I know whence I came, and whither I go; but ye cannot tell whence I come, and whither I go.

15 Ye judge after the flesh; I judge no man.

16 And yet if I judge, my judgment is true: for I am not alone, but I and the Father that sent me.

17 It is also written in your law, that the testimony of two men is true.

18 I am one that bear witness of myself, and the Father that sent me beareth witness of me.

19 Then said they unto him, Where is thy Father? Jesus answered, Ye neither know me, nor my Father: if ye had known me, ye should have known my Father also.

20 These words spake Jesus in the treasury, as he taught in the temple: and no man laid hands on him; for his hour was not yet come.

### Who Art Thou? vv.21-30

21 Then said Jesus again unto them, I go my way, and ye shall seek me, and shall die in your sins: whither I go, ye cannot come.

22 Then said the Jews, Will he kill himself? because he saith, Whither I go, ye cannot come.

23 And he said unto them, Ye are from beneath; I am from above: ye are of this world; I am not of this world.

24 I said therefore unto you, that ye shall die in your sins: for if ye believe not that I am he, ye shall die in your sins.

25 Then said they unto him, Who art thou? And Jesus saith unto them, Even the same that I said unto you from the beginning.

26 I have many things to say and to judge of you: but he that sent me is true; and I speak to the world those things which I have heard of him.

27 They understood not that he spake to them of the Father.

28 Then said Jesus unto them, When ye have lifted up the Son of man, then shall ye know that I am he, and that I do nothing of myself; but as my Father hath taught me, I speak these things.

29 And he that sent me is with me: the Father hath not left me alone; for I do always those things that please him.

30 As he spake these words, many believed on him.

### "My Father" and "your father" vv.31-47

31 Then said Jesus to those Jews which believed on him, If ye continue in my word, then are ye my disciples indeed;

32 And ye shall know the truth, and the truth shall make you free.

33 They answered him, We be Abraham's seed, and were never in bondage to any man: how sayest thou, Ye shall be made free?

34 Jesus answered them, Verily, verily, I say unto you, Whosoever committeth sin is the servant of sin.

35 And the servant abideth not in the house for ever: but the Son abideth ever.

36 If the Son therefore shall make you free, ye shall be free indeed.

out, His standard was the same as His Fathers – a heavenly standard.

8.21-23: The Lord Jesus is claiming to come from heaven.

8.24 'die in your sins' – the serious subject of eternal judgement is now opened up by the Son of God (v21) for all who reject Him.

8.24 'I AM' – the great title of Jehovah was again claimed by Christ.

8.28 'lifted up' – he is referring to His impending death on the cross (see 3.14; 12.32)
'nothing of myself' – a reminder that the Son cannot act in independence of the Father. There is only one God! (see 5.19)

8.29 – a beautiful verse to show the communion and fellowship between the Father and the Son.

8.30-31: These two verses illustrate that to be a believer in the Lord Jesus is to be a disciple.

8.32 Truth liberates (see v36)

8.34 Sin dominates and enslaves (Proverbs 5.21).

8.39 They were hiding behind the name of Abraham and their religion (v33,37,39-40) but missed the God of Abraham.

8.41 'fornication' –they were casting aspersions on the birth of Christ. He was born of a virgin and absolutely pure.

8.42-45 The Jew who refused their Messiah were really accepting the lies of the Devil.

8.46 No one else could ever make this claim apart from Christ. Literally, 'Which one of you can convict me of any sin?'

8.48 – 'devil' means 'demon', 'evil spirit' as opposed to the Devil named in v44.

37 I know that ye are Abraham's seed; but ye seek to kill me, because my word hath no place in you.
38 I speak that which I have seen with my Father: and ye do that which ye have seen with your father.
39 They answered and said unto him, Abraham is our father. Jesus saith unto them, If ye were Abraham's children, ye would do the works of Abraham.
40 But now ye seek to kill me, a man that hath told you the truth, which I have heard of God: this did not Abraham.
41 Ye do the deeds of your father. Then said they to him, We be not born of fornication; we have one Father, even God.
42 Jesus said unto them, If God were your Father, ye would love me: for I proceeded forth and came from God; neither came I of myself, but he sent me.
43 Why do ye not understand my speech? even because ye cannot hear my word.
44 Ye are of your father the devil, and the lusts of your father ye will do. He was a murderer from the beginning, and abode not in the truth, because there is no truth in him. When he speaketh a lie, he speaketh of his own: for he is a liar, and the father of it.
45 And because I tell you the truth, ye believe me not.
46 Which of you convinceth me of sin? And if I say the truth, why do ye not believe me?
47 He that is of God heareth God's words: ye therefore hear them not, because ye are not of God.

***The Lord before Abraham vv.48-59***

48 Then answered the Jews, and said unto him, Say we not well that thou art a Samaritan, and hast a devil?
49 Jesus answered, I have not a devil; but I honour my Father, and ye do dishonour me.
50 And I seek not mine own glory: there is one that seeketh and judgeth.
51 Verily, verily, I say unto you, If a man keep my saying, he shall never see death.
52 Then said the Jews unto him, Now we know that thou hast a devil. Abraham is dead, and the prophets; and thou sayest, If a man keep my saying, he shall never taste of death.
53 Art thou greater than our father Abraham, which is dead? and the prophets are dead: whom makest thou thyself?
54 Jesus answered, If I honour myself, my honour is nothing: it is my Father that honoureth me; of whom ye say, that he is your God:

55 Yet ye have not known him; but I know him: and if I should say, I know him not, I shall be a liar like unto you: but I know him, and keep his saying.
56 Your father Abraham rejoiced to see my day: and he saw it, and was glad.
57 Then said the Jews unto him, Thou art not yet fifty years old, and hast thou seen Abraham?
58 Jesus said unto them, Verily, verily, I say unto you, Before Abraham was, I am.
59 Then took they up stones to cast at him: but Jesus hid himself, and went out of the temple, going through the midst of them, and so passed by.

8.56 – 'Abraham rejoiced to see my day' – Abraham anticipated the coming of the Messiah and when he saw it, he was glad (Genesis 22.17-18; Hebrews 11.9-10).

8.58 Before… I AM. The Lord Jesus is the One who not only predates Abraham but lives in the 'ever present now' outside of time as the great I AM (Exodus 3.14) – He is the eternal unchanging God (see v35 'the Son abides for ever').

8.59 – stones were going to be thrown at Him for what they thought was His blasphemous claim to be God.

A.  Why do you think the woman caught in the act of adultery is recorded in the Bible? vv.1-11.

B.  Read verse 12: What are the other I AM sayings of Christ that you have read so far in John's Gospel? Hint: chapter 6.35 and 8.58.

C.  How can we be liberated from sin? vv.34-36.

_________________________________

_________________________________

_________________________________

_________________________________

# John 9
## The Light of the World Rejected vv.1-41
### *The Sixth Sign: The Blind Man Healed vv.1-7*
1 And as Jesus passed by, he saw a man which was blind from his birth.

2 And his disciples asked him, saying, Master, who did sin, this man, or his parents, that he was born blind?

3 Jesus answered, Neither hath this man sinned, nor his parents: but that the works of God should be made manifest in him.

4 I must work the works of him that sent me, while it is day: the night cometh, when no man can work.

5 As long as I am in the world, I am the light of the world.

6 When he had thus spoken, he spat on the ground, and made clay of the spittle, and he anointed the eyes of the blind man with the clay,

7 And said unto him, Go, wash in the pool of Siloam, (which is by interpretation, Sent.) He went his way therefore, and washed, and came seeing.

### *The Neighbours Question the Man vv.8-12*
8 The neighbours therefore, and they which before had seen him that he was blind, said, Is not this he that sat and begged?

9 Some said, This is he: others said, He is like him: but he said, I am he.

10 Therefore said they unto him, How were thine eyes opened?

11 **He answered and said, A man that is called Jesus made clay, and anointed mine eyes, and said unto me, Go to the pool of Siloam, and wash: and I went and washed, and I received sight**.

12 Then said they unto him, Where is he? He said, I know not.

### *The Pharisees Question the Man vv.13-17*
13 They brought to the Pharisees him that aforetime was blind.

14 And it was the sabbath day when Jesus made the clay, and opened his eyes.

15 Then again the Pharisees also asked him how he had received his sight. He said unto them, He put clay upon mine eyes, and I washed, and do see.

16 Therefore said some of the Pharisees, This man is not of God, because he keepeth not the sabbath day. Others said, How can a man that is a sinner do such miracles? And there was a division among them.

17 They say unto the blind man again, What sayest thou of him, that he hath opened thine eyes? He said, He is a prophet.

9.2-3 There must have been a view by some that disability was a result of sin in a life or in a previous generation. This view is utterly condemned by the Lord Jesus as erroneous. It was widely held by the Pharisees (v34).

9.6 'spittle' means 'saliva'– He was the only man who had no contamination in his saliva as He was sinless.

9.11 The simple testimony of a new believer is more powerful than theological arguments (see v15, 17, 25).

9.13 'aforetime' – means 'beforehand'.

9.22 Religious pressure can cause people to both dismiss the obvious facts (v18, v27) and refuse to state the truth (v22) for fear of the removal of privileges.

9.34 'Cast out' means removed from the synagogue for telling the truth.

9.35 –'Dost' means 'Do'.

***The Pharisees (Jews) Question the Parents vv.18-23***

18 But the Jews did not believe concerning him, that he had been blind, and received his sight, until they called the parents of him that had received his sight.
19 And they asked them, saying, Is this your son, who ye say was born blind? how then doth he now see?
20 His parents answered them and said, We know that this is our son, and that he was born blind:
21 But by what means he now seeth, we know not; or who hath opened his eyes, we know not: he is of age; ask him: he shall speak for himself.
22 These words spake his parents, because they feared the Jews: for the Jews had agreed already, that if any man did confess that he was Christ, he should be put out of the synagogue.
23 Therefore said his parents, He is of age; ask him.

***The Pharisees Question the Man vv.24-34***

24 Then again called they the man that was blind, and said unto him, Give God the praise: we know that this man is a sinner.
25 He answered and said, Whether he be a sinner or no, I know not: one thing I know, that, whereas I was blind, now I see.
26 Then said they to him again, What did he to thee? how opened he thine eyes?
27 He answered them, I have told you already, and ye did not hear: wherefore would ye hear it again? will ye also be his disciples?
28 Then they reviled him, and said, Thou art his disciple; but we are Moses' disciples.
29 We know that God spake unto Moses: as for this fellow, we know not from whence he is.
30 The man answered and said unto them, Why herein is a marvellous thing, that ye know not from whence he is, and yet he hath opened mine eyes.
31 Now we know that God heareth not sinners: but if any man be a worshipper of God, and doeth his will, him he heareth.
32 Since the world began was it not heard that any man opened the eyes of one that was born blind.
33 If this man were not of God, he could do nothing.
34 They answered and said unto him, Thou wast altogether born in sins, and dost thou teach us? And they cast him out.

***The Son Questions the Man vv.35-38***

35 Jesus heard that they had cast him out; and when he had found him, he said unto him, Dost thou believe on the Son of God?
36 He answered and said, Who is he, Lord, that I might believe on him?

37 And Jesus said unto him, Thou hast both seen him, and it is he that talketh with thee.

38 And he said, Lord, I believe. And he worshipped him.

### *The Lord speaks to the Pharisees vv.39-41*

39 And Jesus said, For judgment I am come into this world, that they which see not might see; and that they which see might be made blind.

40 And some of the Pharisees which were with him heard these words, and said unto him, Are we blind also?

41 Jesus said unto them, If ye were blind, ye should have no sin: but now ye say, We see; therefore your sin remaineth.

9.38 The blind man has now more than His physical sight. He has salvation and has come to believe on the Lord Jesus. He has spiritual sight.

9.41 A person that is spiritually blind and knows it can have his or her eyes opened and given spiritual sight. But what can be done for the person who thinks he can see but really does not?

A.  Is suffering the result of sin? vv.1-4.

B.  What was the man's simple testimony? v.25.

C.  When and how did the man receive his spiritual sight? vv.35-38.

D.  What might hinder anyone from receiving spiritual sight? vv.39-41.

______________________________________________

______________________________________________

______________________________________________

______________________________________________

# John 10
## The Good Shepherd Rejected vv.1-42
### *The First Parable vv.1-6*

1 Verily, verily, I say unto you, He that entereth not by the door into the sheepfold, but climbeth up some other way, the same is a thief and a robber.

2 But he that entereth in by the door is the shepherd of the sheep.

3 To him the porter openeth; and the sheep hear his voice: and he calleth his own sheep by name, and leadeth them out.

4 And when he putteth forth his own sheep, he goeth before them, and the sheep follow him: for they know his voice.

5 And a stranger will they not follow, but will flee from him: for they know not the voice of strangers.

6 This parable spake Jesus unto them: but they understood not what things they were which he spake unto them.

### *The Second Parable vv.7-18*

7 Then said Jesus unto them again, Verily, verily, I say unto you, I am the door of the sheep.

8 All that ever came before me are thieves and robbers: but the sheep did not hear them.

9 **I am the door: by me if any man enter in, he shall be saved, and shall go in and out, and find pasture**.

10 **The thief cometh not, but for to steal, and to kill, and to destroy: I am come that they might have life, and that they might have it more abundantly**.

11 **I am the good shepherd: the good shepherd giveth his life for the sheep**.

12 But he that is an hireling, and not the shepherd, whose own the sheep are not, seeth the wolf coming, and leaveth the sheep, and fleeth: and the wolf catcheth them, and scattereth the sheep.

13 The hireling fleeth, because he is an hireling, and careth not for the sheep.

14 I am the good shepherd, and know my sheep, and am known of mine.

15 As the Father knoweth me, even so know I the Father: and I lay down my life for the sheep.

16 And other sheep I have, which are not of this fold: them also I must bring, and they shall hear my voice; and there shall be one fold, and one shepherd.

17 Therefore doth my Father love me, because I lay down my life, that I might take it again.

18 No man taketh it from me, but I lay it down of

10.1 The religious leaders in 9.22 show the characteristics of 'thieves and robbers'.

10.9 The Lord Jesus is the door way to liberty, and fellowship with God and heaven (14.6).

10.10 'more abundantly' means 'life in all its fulness'.

10.14 The Lord Jesus as the Good Shepherd cares for every true believer and will protect them from those who would seek to destroy their spiritual life.

10.15 'even so know I' – What equality! a claim to know the Father even as the Father knows Him.
'I lay down' – what humility and love!

10.16 'other sheep'… 'one fold': the fold of the church and the true Israel will be brought together - Jews and Gentiles – under one Shepherd.

myself. I have power to lay it down, and I have power to take it again. This commandment have I received of my Father.

### The Effect of the Two Parables vv.19-30

19 There was a division therefore again among the Jews for these sayings.

20 And many of them said, He hath a devil, and is mad; why hear ye him?

21 Others said, These are not the words of him that hath a devil. Can a devil open the eyes of the blind?

22 And it was at Jerusalem the feast of the dedication, and it was winter.

23 And Jesus walked in the temple in Solomon's porch.

24 Then came the Jews round about him, and said unto him, How long dost thou make us to doubt? If thou be the Christ, tell us plainly.

25 Jesus answered them, I told you, and ye believed not: the works that I do in my Father's name, they bear witness of me.

26 But ye believe not, because ye are not of my sheep, as I said unto you.

27 My sheep hear my voice, and I know them, and they follow me:

28 And I give unto them eternal life; and they shall never perish, neither shall any man pluck them out of my hand.

29 My Father, which gave them me, is greater than all; and no man is able to pluck them out of my Father's hand.

30 I and my Father are one.

### The Deity of the Son vv.31-42

31 Then the Jews took up stones again to stone him.

32 Jesus answered them, Many good works have I shewed you from my Father; for which of those works do ye stone me?

33 The Jews answered him, saying, For a good work we stone thee not; but for blasphemy; and because that thou, being a man, makest thyself God.

34 Jesus answered them, Is it not written in your law, I said, Ye are gods?

35 If he called them gods, unto whom the word of God came, and the scripture cannot be broken;

36 Say ye of him, whom the Father hath sanctified, and sent into the world, Thou blasphemest; because I said, I am the Son of God?

37 If I do not the works of my Father, believe me not.

38 But if I do, though ye believe not me, believe the works: that ye may know, and believe, that the Father is in me, and I in him.

---

10.22 'feast of the dedication' – this refers to the festival of lights commemorating the day when the temple was restored under the Macabean revolt against the Selucid empire (AD 160-167) on Christmas day.

'Solomon's Porch' – the last remnant of the colonnade of pillars that was still standing in Jerusalem on the east side of Herod's Temple.

10.26 Their unbelief demonstrated that they were not true Christians and not part of His flock.

10.27-28 This is the great truth of the eternal security of the believer. When God gives eternal life He will never take it away again and no one else can either.

10.33 The threat of stoning happened whenever Christ claimed to be God (v30; 8.58-59).

10.34 'gods' - The Hebrew word 'Elohim' was used of God and of the judges of Israel (Psalm 82.6). Here it is referring to the judges.

10.38 The Lord Jesus is saying that His claim is in a different category to the leaders of Israel, He is the One who is in the Father and the Father dwells in Him. As God, He, the Son, is inseparable from the Father.

39 Therefore they sought again to take him: but he escaped out of their hand,
40 And went away again beyond Jordan into the place where John at first baptized; and there he abode.
41 And many resorted unto him, and said, John did no miracle: but all things that John spake of this man were true.
42 And many believed on him there.

A.  In what sense is the Lord Jesus "the Door" and "the Shepherd"? vv.9,11.

B.  Who do the thieves and wolves refer to? vv.1,12.

C.  What does the Lord Jesus give to his sheep? vv.28,29.

D.  Why did the Jews believe they had to kill the Lord Jesus? v.33.

_______________________________________

_______________________________________

_______________________________________

_______________________________________

# John 11
## The Resurrection and the Life Rejected vv.1-57
### *Before the Lord came to Bethany vv.1-16*

1 Now a certain man was sick, named Lazarus, of Bethany, the town of Mary and her sister Martha.
2 (It was that Mary which anointed the Lord with ointment, and wiped his feet with her hair, whose brother Lazarus was sick.)
3 Therefore his sisters sent unto him, saying, Lord, behold, he whom thou lovest is sick.
4 When Jesus heard that, he said, This sickness is not unto death, but for the glory of God, that the Son of God might be glorified thereby.
5 Now Jesus loved Martha, and her sister, and Lazarus.
6 When he had heard therefore that he was sick, he abode two days still in the same place where he was.
7 Then after that saith he to his disciples, Let us go into Judaea again.
8 His disciples say unto him, Master, the Jews of late sought to stone thee; and goest thou thither again?
9 Jesus answered, Are there not twelve hours in the day? If any man walk in the day, he stumbleth not, because he seeth the light of this world.
10 But if a man walk in the night, he stumbleth, because there is no light in him.
11 These things said he: and after that he saith unto them, Our friend Lazarus sleepeth; but I go, that I may awake him out of sleep.
12 Then said his disciples, Lord, if he sleep, he shall do well.
13 Howbeit Jesus spake of his death: but they thought that he had spoken of taking of rest in sleep.
14 Then said Jesus unto them plainly, Lazarus is dead.
15 And I am glad for your sakes that I was not there, to the intent ye may believe; nevertheless let us go unto him.
16 Then said Thomas, which is called Didymus, unto his fellowdisciples, Let us also go, that we may die with him.

### *Martha and Mary meet the Lord vv.17-37*

17 Then when Jesus came, he found that he had lain in the grave four days already.
18 Now Bethany was nigh unto Jerusalem, about fifteen furlongs off:
19 And many of the Jews came to Martha and Mary, to comfort them concerning their brother.
20 Then Martha, as soon as she heard that Jesus was coming, went and met him: but Mary sat still in the house.

11.1 Bethany is only a short distance from Jerusalem (v18).

11.8 'thither' means 'there'.

11.11 The use of the word 'sleep' to speak of believers in death is a common metaphor. The believers in Thessalonica who had died are described as those who 'sleep in Jesus' (1Thess 4. 14).

11.18 '15 furlongs' is just under 2 miles.

11.24 Martha already knew the scriptures taught that there would be a general resurrection when the Messiah came to set up His Kingdom (Dan. 12.2; Isa 26.19).

11.27 Martha understands that the Lord Jesus is the Messiah and has the power to raise the dead now as well as in a coming day. She has come to understand that Jesus is the Christ, the Son of God. It is here that she finds salvation – before she ever saw the miracle of her brother being raised.

11.35 These are immortal words-'Jesus wept'. The tears slowly trickled down the face of the Son of God as He saw what havoc sin had reaped on earth. These were not tears of sentiment or frustration or repentance (He never did or could shed any of those tears) but of deep sorrow and love.

11.39 'Stinketh' – the body was decomposing.
11.40 The Lord taught that believing was seeing and not seeing is believing.
11.41-42 One of the seven recorded prayers to the Father

21 Then said Martha unto Jesus, Lord, if thou hadst been here, my brother had not died.
22 But I know, that even now, whatsoever thou wilt ask of God, God will give it thee.
23 Jesus saith unto her, Thy brother shall rise again.
24 Martha saith unto him, I know that he shall rise again in the resurrection at the last day.
25 **Jesus said unto her, I am the resurrection, and the life: he that believeth in me, though he were dead, yet shall he live**:
26 And whosoever liveth and believeth in me shall never die. Believest thou this?
27 She saith unto him, Yea, Lord: I believe that thou art the Christ, the Son of God, which should come into the world.
28 And when she had so said, she went her way, and called Mary her sister secretly, saying, The Master is come, and calleth for thee.
29 As soon as she heard that, she arose quickly, and came unto him.
30 Now Jesus was not yet come into the town, but was in that place where Martha met him.
31 The Jews then which were with her in the house, and comforted her, when they saw Mary, that she rose up hastily and went out, followed her, saying, She goeth unto the grave to weep there.
32 Then when Mary was come where Jesus was, and saw him, she fell down at his feet, saying unto him, Lord, if thou hadst been here, my brother had not died.
33 When Jesus therefore saw her weeping, and the Jews also weeping which came with her, he groaned in the spirit, and was troubled.
34 And said, Where have ye laid him? They said unto him, Lord, come and see.
35 Jesus wept.
36 Then said the Jews, Behold how he loved him!
37 And some of them said, Could not this man, which opened the eyes of the blind, have caused that even this man should not have died?

***The Seventh Sign: Life from the Grave vv.38-46***

38 Jesus therefore again groaning in himself cometh to the grave. It was a cave, and a stone lay upon it.
39 Jesus said, Take ye away the stone. Martha, the sister of him that was dead, saith unto him, Lord, by this time he stinketh: for he hath been dead four days.
40 Jesus saith unto her, Said I not unto thee, that, if thou wouldest believe, thou shouldest see the glory of God?
41 Then they took away the stone from the place where the dead was laid. And Jesus lifted up his

eyes, and said, Father, I thank thee that thou hast heard me.

42 And I knew that thou hearest me always: but because of the people which stand by I said it, that they may believe that thou hast sent me.

43 And when he thus had spoken, he cried with a loud voice, Lazarus, come forth.

44 And he that was dead came forth, bound hand and foot with graveclothes: and his face was bound about with a napkin. Jesus saith unto them, Loose him, and let him go.

45 Then many of the Jews which came to Mary, and had seen the things which Jesus did, believed on him.

46 But some of them went their ways to the Pharisees, and told them what things Jesus had done.

### The Sanhedrin Plots against the Lord vv.47-57

47 Then gathered the chief priests and the Pharisees a council, and said, What do we? for this man doeth many miracles.

48 If we let him thus alone, all men will believe on him: and the Romans shall come and take away both our place and nation.

49 And one of them, named Caiaphas, being the high priest that same year, said unto them, Ye know nothing at all,

50 Nor consider that it is expedient for us, that one man should die for the people, and that the whole nation perish not.

51 And this spake he not of himself: but being high priest that year, he prophesied that Jesus should die for that nation;

52 And not for that nation only, but that also he should gather together in one the children of God that were scattered abroad.

53 Then from that day forth they took counsel together for to put him to death.

54 Jesus therefore walked no more openly among the Jews; but went thence unto a country near to the wilderness, into a city called Ephraim, and there continued with his disciples.

55 And the Jews' passover was nigh at hand: and many went out of the country up to Jerusalem before the passover, to purify themselves.

56 Then sought they for Jesus, and spake among themselves, as they stood in the temple, What think ye, that he will not come to the feast?

57 Now both the chief priests and the Pharisees had given a commandment, that, if any man knew where he were, he should shew it, that they might take him.

from the Son. We are privileged to listen into the dialogue of the Trinity.

11.44-45 – The power of Christ over death was evident for all to see in the raising a man who had been dead for four days. This caused many to become Christians, but others did not believe despite acknowledging the evidence (v47). They were more concerned with status (v48).

11.51-52 Caiphas would ultimately send Christ to Pilate to be crucified. Yet here, He is prophesying that the Lord Jesus would bring Israel together as one flock. God can use the most evil of men to say the most incredible and truthful things. We will be judged by our own words.

11.55 'Purify'- the paradox is not to be lost on the reader. They are seeking religious purity whilst plotting murder (v53). Religion does not save, it blinds.

A.  What was it the Lord Jesus was asking Martha
    to believe as she already believed in
    resurrection? vv.23-27.

B.  How long has Lazarus been dead by the time
    the Lord Jesus reached the grave? v.39.

C.  Why did the Lord Jesus weep? v.35.

D.  What is the significance of Caiaphas's words?
    vv.49-53.

_______________________________________________

_______________________________________________

_______________________________________________

_______________________________________________

# John 12
## The Corn of Wheat Rejected vv.1-50
### *The Supper in Bethany vv.1-11*
1 Then Jesus six days before the passover came to Bethany, where Lazarus was, which had been dead, whom he raised from the dead.
2 There they made him a supper; and Martha served: but Lazarus was one of them that sat at the table with him.
3 Then took Mary a pound of ointment of spikenard, very costly, and anointed the feet of Jesus, and wiped his feet with her hair: and the house was filled with the odour of the ointment.
4 Then saith one of his disciples, Judas Iscariot, Simon's son, which should betray him,
5 Why was not this ointment sold for three hundred pence, and given to the poor?
6 This he said, not that he cared for the poor; but because he was a thief, and had the bag, and bare what was put therein.
7 Then said Jesus, Let her alone: against the day of my burying hath she kept this.
8 For the poor always ye have with you; but me ye have not always.
9 Much people of the Jews therefore knew that he was there: and they came not for Jesus' sake only, but that they might see Lazarus also, whom he had raised from the dead.
10 But the chief priests consulted that they might put Lazarus also to death;
11 Because that by reason of him many of the Jews went away, and believed on Jesus.
### *The Lord's Triumphant Entry into Jerusalem vv.12-19*
12 On the next day much people that were come to the feast, when they heard that Jesus was coming to Jerusalem,
13 Took branches of palm trees, and went forth to meet him, and cried, Hosanna: Blessed is the King of Israel that cometh in the name of the Lord.
14 And Jesus, when he had found a young ass, sat thereon; as it is written,
15 Fear not, daughter of Sion: behold, thy King cometh, sitting on an ass's colt.
16 These things understood not his disciples at the first: but when Jesus was glorified, then remembered they that these things were written of him, and that they had done these things unto him.
17 The people therefore that was with him when he called Lazarus out of his grave, and raised him from the dead, bare record.

12.1 'Six days' – The next nine chapters deal with the last six days of the life of Christ on earth. The Lord Jesus would die on Passover as had been predicted for thousands of years (Exodus 12). John's gospel starts with a week (John 1-2) and ends with a week in the life of the Lord. This week is often called passion week.

12. 3 'very costly' – Judas values the ointment at 300 pence (v5) which would be the annual salary for a labouring man. Mary poured her life savings out on Christ. She was keeping it for his burial (v7) but she wanted to show her love and devotion to Him in His life- and knew she would hardly get another chance. Her worship was appreciated in heaven.

12.10-11 These words show the blindness of unbelief. They were plotting now to kill Lazarus as so many were coming to follow Christ because of the resurrection of Lazarus. The problem outlined here is the will of humans to believe, not the intellectual evidence to believe.

12. 13 'Hosannah' means 'save us' 'King of Israel' – on this day they acknowledged the Lord Jesus as Messiah and King. In a few days, when the popularity subsided, they would regard Him as a criminal crying "crucify Him". Such is the fickleness of the human race.

12.16 'When Jesus was glorified' i.e. after His resurrection He ascended into heaven on the fortieth day as recorded in Acts chapter 1 from the Mount of Olives. He is now alive in heaven.

12.21 Philip is good at finding people (1.45) who then become Christians. He must have been approachable.

12.24 The Lord is using the illustration of seed falling into the ground, dying, germinating and growing up and then being harvested as a picture of His death, burial and resurrection.

12.25 The Lord is teaching that the pathway of discipleship was the pathway of self denial.

12.27 'Save me from this hour' - the holy Soul of Christ recoiled from going to Calvary as the sin bearer and yet He went to accomplish the will of the Father.

12.31'the prince of this world' is another name for the Devil.

12.33 He was referring to his death by crucifixion and being lifted up and impaled on a cross. This had been predicted over 700 years earlier in Psalm 22 before the Romans existed or they had invented the form of capital punishment called crucifixion.

18 For this cause the people also met him, for that they heard that he had done this miracle.

19 The Pharisees therefore said among themselves, Perceive ye how ye prevail nothing? behold, the world is gone after him.

### The Lord's Answer to the Greeks' Desire to See Him vv.20-36

20 And there were certain Greeks among them that came up to worship at the feast:

21 The same came therefore to Philip, which was of Bethsaida of Galilee, and desired him, saying, Sir, we would see Jesus.

22 Philip cometh and telleth Andrew: and again Andrew and Philip tell Jesus.

23 And Jesus answered them, saying, The hour is come, that the Son of man should be glorified.

24 Verily, verily, I say unto you, Except a corn of wheat fall into the ground and die, it abideth alone: but if it die, it bringeth forth much fruit.

25 He that loveth his life shall lose it; and he that hateth his life in this world shall keep it unto life eternal.

26 If any man serve me, let him follow me; and where I am, there shall also my servant be: if any man serve me, him will my Father honour.

27 Now is my soul troubled; and what shall I say? Father, save me from this hour: but for this cause came I unto this hour.

28 Father, glorify thy name. Then came there a voice from heaven, saying, I have both glorified it, and will glorify it again.

29 The people therefore, that stood by, and heard it, said that it thundered: others said, An angel spake to him.

30 Jesus answered and said, This voice came not because of me, but for your sakes.

31 Now is the judgment of this world: now shall the prince of this world be cast out.

32 And I, if I be lifted up from the earth, will draw all men unto me.

33 This he said, signifying what death he should die.

34 The people answered him, We have heard out of the law that Christ abideth for ever: and how sayest thou, The Son of man must be lifted up? who is this Son of man?

35 Then Jesus said unto them, Yet a little while is the light with you. Walk while ye have the light, lest darkness come upon you: for he that walketh in darkness knoweth not whither he goeth.

36 While ye have light, believe in the light, that ye

may be the children of light. These things spake Jesus, and departed, and did hide himself from them.

### Unbelief Illustrated from the Prophecy of Isaiah vv.37-43

37 But though he had done so many miracles before them, yet they believed not on him:

38 That the saying of Esaias the prophet might be fulfilled, which he spake, Lord, who hath believed our report? and to whom hath the arm of the Lord been revealed?

39 Therefore they could not believe, because that Esaias said again,

40 He hath blinded their eyes, and hardened their heart; that they should not see with their eyes, nor understand with their heart, and be converted, and I should heal them.

41 These things said Esaias, when he saw his glory, and spake of him.

42 Nevertheless among the chief rulers also many believed on him; but because of the Pharisees they did not confess him, lest they should be put out of the synagogue:

43 For they loved the praise of men more than the praise of God.

### Summary of the Lord's Teaching in John's Gospel vv.44-50

44 Jesus cried and said, He that believeth on me, believeth not on me, but on him that sent me.

45 And he that seeth me seeth him that sent me.

46 I am come a light into the world, that whosoever believeth on me should not abide in darkness.

47 And if any man hear my words, and believe not, I judge him not: for I came not to judge the world, but to save the world.

48 He that rejecteth me, and receiveth not my words, hath one that judgeth him: the word that I have spoken, the same shall judge him in the last day.

49 For I have not spoken of myself; but the Father which sent me, he gave me a commandment, what I should say, and what I should speak.

50 And I know that his commandment is life everlasting: whatsoever I speak therefore, even as the Father said unto me, so I speak.

12.39 Unbelief is not based on a lack of evidence but the stubbornness of the will and the fear of other people and popularity (see 42-43).

12.41 Esaias is the Greek transliteration of Isaiah, the prophet. This is an astonishing proof of the deity of Christ. Read Isaiah 6.1-3.

12.49-50 The Lord Jesus is claiming that He spoke the same message and the same words and utterances as the Father and He spoke them in the same manner, with the same motive.

A.  What value did Judas Iscariot put on Christ compared to Mary? vv.3-8.

B.  What concerns did the Pharisees have when the Lord arrived in Jerusalem on Palm Sunday? vv.10-19.

C.  What is the significance of the corn of wheat? v.24.

D.  What was the Lord referring to when He said He would be lifted up? v.32.

______________________________________

______________________________________

______________________________________

______________________________________

______________________________________

# John 13

**The Upper Room: The Son's Activity vv.1-38**
*The Son-to be called Lord vv.1-17*

1 Now before the feast of the passover, when Jesus knew that his hour was come that he should depart out of this world unto the Father, having loved his own which were in the world, he loved them unto the end.

2 And supper being ended, the devil having now put into the heart of Judas Iscariot, Simon's son, to betray him;

3 Jesus knowing that the Father had given all things into his hands, and that he was come from God, and went to God;

4 He riseth from supper, and laid aside his garments; and took a towel, and girded himself.

5 After that he poureth water into a bason, and began to wash the disciples' feet, and to wipe them with the towel wherewith he was girded.

6 Then cometh he to Simon Peter: and Peter saith unto him, Lord, dost thou wash my feet?

7 Jesus answered and said unto him, What I do thou knowest not now; but thou shalt know hereafter.

8 Peter saith unto him, Thou shalt never wash my feet. Jesus answered him, If I wash thee not, thou hast no part with me.

9 Simon Peter saith unto him, Lord, not my feet only, but also my hands and my head.

10 Jesus saith to him, He that is washed needeth not save to wash his feet, but is clean every whit: and ye are clean, but not all.

11 For he knew who should betray him; therefore said he, Ye are not all clean.

12 So after he had washed their feet, and had taken his garments, and was set down again, he said unto them, Know ye what I have done to you?

13 Ye call me Master and Lord: and ye say well; for so I am.

14 If I then, your Lord and Master, have washed your feet; ye also ought to wash one another's feet.

15 For I have given you an example, that ye should do as I have done to you.

16 Verily, verily, I say unto you, The servant is not greater than his lord; neither he that is sent greater than he that sent him.

17 If ye know these things, happy are ye if ye do them.

*The Son-to be Betrayed vv.44-50*

18 I speak not of you all: I know whom I have chosen: but that the scripture may be fulfilled, He that eateth bread with me hath lifted up his heel against me.

13.4 This is a beautiful picture of the truth of verse 3. He, as God, left heaven and came down in the clothing of a servant to serve and meet the needs of men and woman.

13.15 'as I have done' – not so much 'what I have done'. He is teaching his disciples the great principle of humility in their service to one another, and not establishing another ritual.

13.18 The Lord Jesus is predicting the betrayal by Judas Iscariot and stating that this fulfills in part Psalm 41.9 (v18).

13.23 John is referring to Himself 'the disciple whom Jesus loved'. He was lying on a couch as was the custom at that time when eating and the back of His head reclined back on the chest of the Christ of God. He could hear the very heart beat of Christ.

13.26 'the sop' means a special morsel of food normally given to the most honoured guest. The Lord treated Judas Iscariot with the upmost respect and yet indicated most clearly to him the awfulness of his sin. Judas instead of repenting ate the sop, sealing his doom and became indwelt by Satan.

13.28-29 Despite the clear statements by Christ the disciples are still in confusion about the true character of Judas Iscariot.

13.36 'Whither goes thou?' means 'where are you going?' The Lord Jesus was speaking of going to heaven.

19 Now I tell you before it come, that, when it is come to pass, ye may believe that I am he.

20 Verily, verily, I say unto you, He that receiveth whomsoever I send receiveth me; and he that receiveth me receiveth him that sent me.

21 When Jesus had thus said, he was troubled in spirit, and testified, and said, Verily, verily, I say unto you, that one of you shall betray me.

22 Then the disciples looked one on another, doubting of whom he spake.

23 Now there was leaning on Jesus' bosom one of his disciples, whom Jesus loved.

24 Simon Peter therefore beckoned to him, that he should ask who it should be of whom he spake.

25 He then lying on Jesus' breast saith unto him, Lord, who is it?

26 Jesus answered, He it is, to whom I shall give a sop, when I have dipped it. And when he had dipped the sop, he gave it to Judas Iscariot, the son of Simon.

27 And after the sop Satan entered into him. Then said Jesus unto him, That thou doest, do quickly.

28 Now no man at the table knew for what intent he spake this unto him.

29 For some of them thought, because Judas had the bag, that Jesus had said unto him, Buy those things that we have need of against the feast; or, that he should give something to the poor.

30 He then having received the sop went immediately out: and it was night.

### The Son-to be Glorified vv.31-35

31 Therefore, when he was gone out, Jesus said, Now is the Son of man glorified, and God is glorified in him.

32 If God be glorified in him, God shall also glorify him in himself, and shall straightway glorify him.

33 Little children, yet a little while I am with you. Ye shall seek me: and as I said unto the Jews, Whither I go, ye cannot come; so now I say to you.

34 A new commandment I give unto you, That ye love one another; as I have loved you, that ye also love one another.

35 By this shall all men know that ye are my disciples, if ye have love one to another.

### The Son-to be Denied vv.36-38

36 Simon Peter said unto him, Lord, whither goest thou? Jesus answered him, Whither I go, thou canst not follow me now; but thou shalt follow me afterwards.

37 Peter said unto him, Lord, why cannot I follow thee now? I will lay down my life for thy sake.

38 Jesus answered him, Wilt thou lay down thy life for my sake? Verily, verily, I say unto thee, The cock shall not crow, till thou hast denied me thrice.

A.  Why did the Lord Jesus take a basin and towel and wash the disciples feet? vv.1-17.

B.  How does the Lord Jesus treat Judas Iscariot? vv.18-30.

C.  What is the new commandment? vv.31-35.

D.  How would Peter know that He had denied His Lord? vv.36-38.

_______________________________________________

_______________________________________________

_______________________________________________

_______________________________________________

# John 14
## The Upper Room: The Son's Teaching about the Comforter vv.1-31
### The Father's House on High vv.1-4
1 Let not your heart be troubled: ye believe in God, believe also in me.

2 In my Father's house are many mansions: if it were not so, I would have told you. I go to prepare a place for you.

3 And if I go and prepare a place for you, I will come again, and receive you unto myself; that where I am, there ye may be also.

4 And whither I go ye know, and the way ye know.

### The Question of Thomas vv.5-7
5 Thomas saith unto him, Lord, we know not whither thou goest; and how can we know the way?

6 **Jesus saith unto him, I am the way, the truth, and the life: no man cometh unto the Father, but by me**.

7 If ye had known me, ye should have known my Father also: and from henceforth ye know him, and have seen him.

### The Statement of Philip vv.8-21
8 Philip saith unto him, Lord, show us the Father, and it sufficeth us.

9 Jesus saith unto him, Have I been so long time with you, and yet hast thou not known me, Philip? he that hath seen me hath seen the Father; and how sayest thou then, Show us the Father?

10 Believest thou not that I am in the Father, and the Father in me? the words that I speak unto you I speak not of myself: but the Father that dwelleth in me, he doeth the works.

11 Believe me that I am in the Father, and the Father in me: or else believe me for the very works' sake.

12 Verily, verily, I say unto you, He that believeth on me, the works that I do shall he do also; and greater works than these shall he do; because I go unto my Father.

13 And whatsoever ye shall ask in my name, that will I do, that the Father may be glorified in the Son.

14 If ye shall ask any thing in my name, I will do it.

15 If ye love me, keep my commandments.

16 And I will pray the Father, and he shall give you another Comforter, that he may abide with you for ever;

17 Even the Spirit of truth; whom the world cannot receive, because it seeth him not, neither knoweth him: but ye know him; for he dwelleth with you, and shall be in you.

---

**14.2** 'The Father's House' is another name for heaven. There is a place prepared for all who trust the Lord Jesus as Saviour.

**14.3** The Lord Jesus is coming again for His people.

**14.6** The Lord Jesus claims to be the only way to the Father. There is one way to salvation.

**14.8** Phillip is saying we shall be satisfied just to see the Father.

**14.9** The Lord Jesus tells Him to see the Son is to see the Father, as the Son is God, and God is revealed through Him to the human race.

**14.10** 'doeth' means 'does'. This verse shows that you cannot separate the Father from the Son. There is only one God.

**14.12** 'greater works' – this cannot mean greater in essence as His works were the works of God, but it does means greater in scope as His ministry was limited both in time and in geography whilst on earth.

**14.15-26** The Lord Jesus is predicting the coming of the Holy Spirit into the lives of God's people after He has ascended to the Father (see 7.39).

18 I will not leave you comfortless: I will come to you.

19 Yet a little while, and the world seeth me no more; but ye see me: because I live, ye shall live also.

20 At that day ye shall know that I am in my Father, and ye in me, and I in you.

21 He that hath my commandments, and keepeth them, he it is that loveth me: and he that loveth me shall be loved of my Father, and I will love him, and will manifest myself to him.

### The Question of Judas (not Iscariot) vv.22-31

22 Judas saith unto him, not Iscariot, Lord, how is it that thou wilt manifest thyself unto us, and not unto the world?

23 Jesus answered and said unto him, If a man love me, he will keep my words: and my Father will love him, and we will come unto him, and make our abode with him.

24 He that loveth me not keepeth not my sayings: and the word which ye hear is not mine, but the Father's which sent me.

25 These things have I spoken unto you, being yet present with you.

26 But the Comforter, which is the Holy Ghost, whom the Father will send in my name, he shall teach you all things, and bring all things to your remembrance, whatsoever I have said unto you.

27 **Peace I leave with you, my peace I give unto you: not as the world giveth, give I unto you. Let not your heart be troubled, neither let it be afraid**.

28 Ye have heard how I said unto you, I go away, and come again unto you. If ye loved me, ye would rejoice, because I said, I go unto the Father: for my Father is greater than I.

29 And now I have told you before it come to pass, that, when it is come to pass, ye might believe.

30 Hereafter I will not talk much with you: for the prince of this world cometh, and hath nothing in me.

31 But that the world may know that I love the Father; and as the Father gave me commandment, even so I do. Arise, let us go hence.

14.20-21 These incredible words reflect the intimacy of God in the life of someone who has accepted salvation in Christ.

14.28 Not greater personally or greater essentially as the Lord Jesus is God but greater officially. The Lord Jesus had taken the position and role of a servant to the Father (v31) and had come to earth to serve Him and do His will.

14.30 'Nothing in me' – there was nothing in the life of Christ that could even respond to Satan's evil suggestions. The Lord Jesus "did no sin" (1peter 2.22) and "knew no sin" (2Cor. 5.21) and "in Him is no sin" (1John 3.5) and He could not be tested by sin (Heb. 4.15).

A.  How can we get to the Father's House
in Heaven? vv.1-6.

B.  How can we see the Father God? vv.7-11.

C.  In what sense could the disciples works be
greater than the Lord's? v.12.

D.  In what sense is the peace given by the Lord
different to the world's peace? v.27.

_______________________________________

_______________________________________

_______________________________________

_______________________________________

# John 15
**The Way to Gethsemane: The Son's Teaching about Fruitfulness vv.1-27**
*The True Vine: its Branches and its Fruit vv.1-8*
1 **I am the true vine, and my Father is the husbandman**.
2 Every branch in me that beareth not fruit he taketh away: and every branch that beareth fruit, he purgeth it, that it may bring forth more fruit.
3 Now ye are clean through the word which I have spoken unto you.
4 Abide in me, and I in you. As the branch cannot bear fruit of itself, except it abide in the vine; no more can ye, except ye abide in me.
5 I am the vine, ye are the branches: He that abideth in me, and I in him, the same bringeth forth much fruit: for without me ye can do nothing.
6 If a man abide not in me, he is cast forth as a branch, and is withered; and men gather them, and cast them into the fire, and they are burned.
7 If ye abide in me, and my words abide in you, ye shall ask what ye will, and it shall be done unto you.
8 Herein is my Father glorified, that ye bear much fruit; so shall ye be my disciples.
*Love, the First Fruit of the Spirit in the Believer vv.9-16*
9 As the Father hath loved me, so have I loved you: continue ye in my love.
10 If ye keep my commandments, ye shall abide in my love; even as I have kept my Father's commandments, and abide in his love.
11 These things have I spoken unto you, that my joy might remain in you, and that your joy might be full.
12 This is my commandment, That ye love one another, as I have loved you.
13 Greater love hath no man than this, that a man lay down his life for his friends.
14 Ye are my friends, if ye do whatsoever I command you.
15 Henceforth I call you not servants; for the servant knoweth not what his lord doeth: but I have called you friends; for all things that I have heard of my Father I have made known unto you.
16 Ye have not chosen me, but I have chosen you, and ordained you, that ye should go and bring forth fruit, and that your fruit should remain: that whatsoever ye shall ask of the Father in my name, he may give it you.

15.1 The vine speaks of joy in the scriptures. He is the true vine the only true source of joy for all the human race.
'Husbandman' - the dresser of the vine.

15.4 'abide in Me' - This illustration is all about enjoying fellowship with Christ and producing fruit out of this enjoyment of intimate fellowship. This is not talking about our salvation in Christ which is based upon his death and resurrection but the active enjoyment of what Christians have been brought into.

15.13 Love is sacrificial.

15.15 The relationship disciples have with Christ is above servants and is called friendship.

15.16-18 Andrew, Peter, James and John and all the disciples were chosen to be fruitful for God and this would be seen in their love for one another. They were going to endure incredible persecution, however.

### *Hate, the Fruit of the Flesh in the Unbeliever vv.17-27*

17 These things I command you, that ye love one another.

18 If the world hate you, ye know that it hated me before it hated you.

19 If ye were of the world, the world would love his own: but because ye are not of the world, but I have chosen you out of the world, therefore the world hateth you.

20 Remember the word that I said unto you, The servant is not greater than his lord. If they have persecuted me, they will also persecute you; if they have kept my saying, they will keep yours also.

21 But all these things will they do unto you for my name's sake, because they know not him that sent me.

22 If I had not come and spoken unto them, they had not had sin: but now they have no cloak for their sin.

23 He that hateth me hateth my Father also.

24 If I had not done among them the works which none other man did, they had not had sin: but now have they both seen and hated both me and my Father.

25 But this cometh to pass, that the word might be fulfilled that is written in their law, They hated me without a cause.

26 But when the Comforter is come, whom I will send unto you from the Father, even the Spirit of truth, which proceedeth from the Father, he shall testify of me:

27 And ye also shall bear witness, because ye have been with me from the beginning.

15.26-27 The function of the Holy Spirit is to testify of the Lord Jesus. A divine person helps us in our enjoyment of our Christian faith and helps us to testify for Christ.

A.  List the "I Am" statements of Christ?
    6.35; 8.12,58; 10.9,11; 11.25; 14.6.

B.  What does the Lord call His disciples in verse 13?

C.  What should disciples of Christ expect? vv.17-25.

D.  Who helps Christians to testify for Christ?
    vv.26-27.

___________________________________________

___________________________________________

___________________________________________

___________________________________________

# John 16

**The Way to Gethsemane: The Son's Teaching about His Departure vv.1-33**

*Aspects of Persecution vv.1-4*

1 These things have I spoken unto you, that ye should not be offended.

2 They shall put you out of the synagogues: yea, the time cometh, that whosoever killeth you will think that he doeth God service.

3 And these things will they do unto you, because they have not known the Father, nor me.

4 But these things have I told you, that when the time shall come, ye may remember that I told you of them. And these things I said not unto you at the beginning, because I was with you.

*The Work of the Holy Spirit vv.5-15*

5 But now I go my way to him that sent me; and none of you asketh me, Whither goest thou?

6 But because I have said these things unto you, sorrow hath filled your heart.

7 Nevertheless I tell you the truth; It is expedient for you that I go away: for if I go not away, the Comforter will not come unto you; but if I depart, I will send him unto you.

8 **And when he is come, he will reprove the world of sin, and of righteousness, and of judgment**:

9 Of sin, because they believe not on me;

10 Of righteousness, because I go to my Father, and ye see me no more;

11 Of judgment, because the prince of this world is judged.

12 I have yet many things to say unto you, but ye cannot bear them now.

13 Howbeit when he, the Spirit of truth, is come, he will guide you into all truth: for he shall not speak of himself; but whatsoever he shall hear, that shall he speak: and he will shew you things to come.

14 He shall glorify me: for he shall receive of mine, and shall shew it unto you.

15 All things that the Father hath are mine: therefore said I, that he shall take of mine, and shall shew it unto you.

*The Lord's Statements Regarding His Death and Resurrection vv.16-22*

16 A little while, and ye shall not see me: and again, a little while, and ye shall see me, because I go to the Father.

17 Then said some of his disciples among themselves, What is this that he saith unto us, A little while, and ye shall not see me: and again, a little while, and ye shall see me: and, Because I go to the Father?

---

16.5 Now they did understand the answer to their question in 14.5 - He was going to heaven with the Father (v16) and so they were sad.

16.7 'expedient' means 'necessary'. The Holy Spirit would only come to them after the Lord Jesus had ascended to the Father.

16.8 'reprove' means 'convict'.

16.12-15 One of the roles of the Holy Spirit would be to tell the apostles the words of Christ that they would not be able to take in at that time (v12) and so complete the canon of holy scripture.

18 They said therefore, What is this that he saith, A little while? we cannot tell what he saith.

19 Now Jesus knew that they were desirous to ask him, and said unto them, Do ye enquire among yourselves of that I said, A little while, and ye shall not see me: and again, a little while, and ye shall see me?

20 Verily, verily, I say unto you, That ye shall weep and lament, but the world shall rejoice: and ye shall be sorrowful, but your sorrow shall be turned into joy.

21 A woman when she is in travail hath sorrow, because her hour is come: but as soon as she is delivered of the child, she remembereth no more the anguish, for joy that a man is born into the world.

22 And ye now therefore have sorrow: but I will see you again, and your heart shall rejoice, and your joy no man taketh from you.

### Prayer in His Name to the Father vv.23-33

23 And in that day ye shall ask me nothing. Verily, verily, I say unto you, Whatsoever ye shall ask the Father in my name, he will give it you.

24 Hitherto have ye asked nothing in my name: ask, and ye shall receive, that your joy may be full.

25 These things have I spoken unto you in proverbs: but the time cometh, when I shall no more speak unto you in proverbs, but I shall shew you plainly of the Father.

26 At that day ye shall ask in my name: and I say not unto you, that I will pray the Father for you:

27 For the Father himself loveth you, because ye have loved me, and have believed that I came out from God.

28 I came forth from the Father, and am come into the world: again, I leave the world, and go to the Father.

29 His disciples said unto him, Lo, now speakest thou plainly, and speakest no proverb.

30 Now are we sure that thou knowest all things, and needest not that any man should ask thee: by this we believe that thou camest forth from God.

31 Jesus answered them, Do ye now believe?

32 Behold, the hour cometh, yea, is now come, that ye shall be scattered, every man to his own, and shall leave me alone: and yet I am not alone, because the Father is with me.

33 These things I have spoken unto you, that in me ye might have peace. In the world ye shall have tribulation: but be of good cheer; I have overcome the world.

16.20 The first 'little while' (when they shall not see Him) is explained in this verse – it will not be long till he dies for the sins of the world; a matters of days.

16.21-22 The second "little while' (when they shall see him) is explained in these verses as he speaks of the period of his burial and then resurrection from the dead.

16.23 'That day' – speaks of the present day. During this 'little while' when He is in heaven we pray to the Father in His Name, awaiting His return (John 14.1-3).

16.29 'Lo' means 'See'.

A.  When did the Holy Spirit come down to earth? v.7.

B.  What does the Holy Spirit do? vv.8-15.

C.  How should we pray today? v.23.

_______________________________________________

_______________________________________________

_______________________________________________

_______________________________________________

# John 17
**The Way to Gethsemane: The Son in the Sanctuary vv.1-26**
***The Son's Eternal Relationship with the Father vv.1-5***

1 These words spake Jesus, and lifted up his eyes to heaven, and said, Father, the hour is come; glorify thy Son, that thy Son also may glorify thee:

2 As thou hast given him power over all flesh, that he should give eternal life to as many as thou hast given him.

3 **And this is life eternal, that they might know thee the only true God, and Jesus Christ, whom thou hast sent**.

4 I have glorified thee on the earth: I have finished the work which thou gavest me to do.

5 And now, O Father, glorify thou me with thine own self with the glory which I had with thee before the world was.

***Prayer on Behalf of His Disciples Who Would be Left vv.6-19***

6 I have manifested thy name unto the men which thou gavest me out of the world: thine they were, and thou gavest them me; and they have kept thy word.

7 Now they have known that all things whatsoever thou hast given me are of thee.

8 For I have given unto them the words which thou gavest me; and they have received them, and have known surely that I came out from thee, and they have believed that thou didst send me.

9 I pray for them: I pray not for the world, but for them which thou hast given me; for they are thine.

10 And all mine are thine, and thine are mine; and I am glorified in them.

11 And now I am no more in the world, but these are in the world, and I come to thee. Holy Father, keep through thine own name those whom thou hast given me, that they may be one, as we are.

12 While I was with them in the world, I kept them in thy name: those that thou gavest me I have kept, and none of them is lost, but the son of perdition; that the scripture might be fulfilled.

13 And now come I to thee; and these things I speak in the world, that they might have my joy fulfilled in themselves.

14 I have given them thy word; and the world hath hated them, because they are not of the world, even as I am not of the world.

17.4 The Lord Jesus is speaking in the past tense here (see v11). The work of Calvary was still before Him but in this anticipatory prayer it is as if it is all complete. He was and is the One who finished completely the Father's will and everything that was necessary in order for men and woman to have sins forgiven and everlasting life.

17.5 The Lord Jesus, as God, has an inherent glory, which He had before the foundation of the world (v5; v24). He also had an acquired glory on earth in becoming a man and serving His Father (v4) which He has now taken into heaven. He also will have a future glory with the Father in heaven (v5).

17.11 Praying that the unity of the Trinity might be reflected in the Apostles.

17.12 'son of perdition' is Judas Iscariot. 'Perdition' means 'destruction'.

17.13 Praying for the joy of the Apostles.

17.15 Praying for the preservation of the Apostles.

15 I pray not that thou shouldest take them out of the world, but that thou shouldest keep them from the evil.
16 They are not of the world, even as I am not of the world.

17.17 Praying for the separation and sanctification of the Apostles.

17 Sanctify them through thy truth: thy word is truth.
18 As thou hast sent me into the world, even so have I also sent them into the world.
19 And for their sakes I sanctify myself, that they also might be sanctified through the truth.

***Prayer on Behalf of All Subsequent Converts vv.20-26***

17.20 Praying for the preaching of the Apostles – for unity amongst believers.
17.21 Praying for the salvation of the world.

20 Neither pray I for these alone, but for them also which shall believe on me through their word;
21 That they all may be one; as thou, Father, art in me, and I in thee, that they also may be one in us: that the world may believe that thou hast sent me.
22 And the glory which thou gavest me I have given them; that they may be one, even as we are one:
23 I in them, and thou in me, that they may be made perfect in one; and that the world may know that thou hast sent me, and hast loved them, as thou hast loved me.

17.24 Praying for the glory of the Apostles.

24 Father, I will that they also, whom thou hast given me, be with me where I am; that they may behold my glory, which thou hast given me: for thou lovedst me before the foundation of the world.
25 O righteous Father, the world hath not known thee: but I have known thee, and these have known that thou hast sent me.

17.26 Praying that the love of God may be in the Apostles.

26 And I have declared unto them thy name, and will declare it: that the love wherewith thou hast loved me may be in them, and I in them.

## *Reflective Questions and Notes*

A.  What is life eternal? v.3.

B.  What did the Lord Jesus finish? v.4.

C.  What did the Lord Jesus pray for? vv.15-26.

___________________________________________

___________________________________________

___________________________________________

___________________________________________

# John 18
## The Betrayal by Judas and the Denial by Peter vv.1-27
### The Betrayal of the Lord by Judas vv.1-11

18.1 'Cedron' also called 'Kidron' a stream which appeared in winter in the valley between Jerusalem and the Mount of Olives on the East of the city.
'garden' – other gospels call it the garden of Gethsemane (Garden of olives).

18.3 Lanterns – a light.
Torches – normally only used of lights which were fed with oil.

18.4 'Whom seek ye?' means 'Who are you looking for?'

18.5 'I AM' is the Name of God (Exodus 3.14). The Lord Jesus claimed to be God.
18.6 Involuntarily, they went backwards and then fell forward on their face in obeisance, prostrate before Him. What power!

18.11 John does not record, unlike Luke, how he healed Malchus' servant's ear instead he concentrates on describing the Lord's rebuke to Peter that he had not come to use physical force but to drink the cup of sorrow and die for the world. The undrawn sword is the ministry of Christ.

18.14 see 11.49-52.

18.15 'another disciple' is John, characteristically withholding his name.

1 When Jesus had spoken these words, he went forth with his disciples over the brook Cedron, where was a garden, into the which he entered, and his disciples.
2 And Judas also, which betrayed him, knew the place: for Jesus ofttimes resorted thither with his disciples.
3 Judas then, having received a band of men and officers from the chief priests and Pharisees, cometh thither with lanterns and torches and weapons.
4 Jesus therefore, knowing all things that should come upon him, went forth, and said unto them, Whom seek ye?
5 They answered him, Jesus of Nazareth. Jesus saith unto them, I am he. And Judas also, which betrayed him, stood with them.
6 As soon then as he had said unto them, I am he, they went backward, and fell to the ground.
7 Then asked he them again, Whom seek ye? And they said, Jesus of Nazareth.
8 Jesus answered, I have told you that I am he: if therefore ye seek me, let these go their way:
9 That the saying might be fulfilled, which he spake, Of them which thou gavest me have I lost none.
10 Then Simon Peter having a sword drew it, and smote the high priest's servant, and cut off his right ear. The servant's name was Malchus.
11 Then said Jesus unto Peter, Put up thy sword into the sheath: the cup which my Father hath given me, shall I not drink it?

### The Lord Taken, and Peter's First Denial vv.12-18
12 Then the band and the captain and officers of the Jews took Jesus, and bound him,
13 And led him away to Annas first; for he was father in law to Caiaphas, which was the high priest that same year.
14 Now Caiaphas was he, which gave counsel to the Jews, that it was expedient that one man should die for the people.
15 And Simon Peter followed Jesus, and so did another disciple: that disciple was known unto the high priest, and went in with Jesus into the palace of the high priest.
16 But Peter stood at the door without. Then went out that other disciple, which was known unto the

high priest, and spake unto her that kept the door, and brought in Peter.

17 Then saith the damsel that kept the door unto Peter, Art not thou also one of this man's disciples? He saith, I am not.

18 And the servants and officers stood there, who had made a fire of coals; for it was cold: and they warmed themselves: and Peter stood with them, and warmed himself.

### The Lord before the High Priest, and Peter's Further Denials vv.19-27

19 The high priest then asked Jesus of his disciples, and of his doctrine.

20 Jesus answered him, I spake openly to the world; I ever taught in the synagogue, and in the temple, whither the Jews always resort; and in secret have I said nothing.

21 Why askest thou me? ask them which heard me, what I have said unto them: behold, they know what I said.

22 And when he had thus spoken, one of the officers which stood by struck Jesus with the palm of his hand, saying, Answerest thou the high priest so?

23 Jesus answered him, If I have spoken evil, bear witness of the evil: but if well, why smitest thou me?

24 Now Annas had sent him bound unto Caiaphas the high priest.

25 And Simon Peter stood and warmed himself. They said therefore unto him, Art not thou also one of his disciples? He denied it, and said, I am not.

26 One of the servants of the high priest, being his kinsman whose ear Peter cut off, saith, Did not I see thee in the garden with him?

27 Peter then denied again: and immediately the cock crew.

### The Lord before Pilate 18.28 to 19.16

### Pilate out to the Jews vv.28-32

28 Then led they Jesus from Caiaphas unto the hall of judgment: and it was early; and they themselves went not into the judgment hall, lest they should be defiled; but that they might eat the passover.

29 Pilate then went out unto them, and said, What accusation bring ye against this man?

30 They answered and said unto him, If he were not a malefactor, we would not have delivered him up unto thee.

31 Then said Pilate unto them, Take ye him, and judge him according to your law. The Jews therefore said unto him, It is not lawful for us to put any man to death:

18.20 'resort' means 'come together'.

18.22 surely the slap reverberated around the courts of heaven as puny man dared to raise their hand to the face of Christ.

18.28 'lest they should be defiled' – what irony! They wanted to be ceremonially clean but had no conscience about murdering a perfect man. Religion has always allowed gross sin to sit side by side with legalistic rules.

18.29-31 Pilate asks what the charges are but they do not offer any specific charge other than a general description of Him as an evil doer(malefactor). They then request the death sentence without still detailing any charge.

18.36-37 The Lord Jesus makes it clear that He is a King and a King before He was born.

18.38 Pilate turn away after he asked this question. If only he had remained to hear the answer. Read John 14.6.

18.38-40 Pilate knows the Lord Jesus is innocent of all charges and yet he is not interested in justice but a political solution. He is perhaps not expecting the hatred of the crowd to choose the release of the murderer Barabbas rather than the Christ.

32 That the saying of Jesus might be fulfilled, which he spake, signifying what death he should die.

***Pilate into the Judgment Hall vv.33-38***

33 Then Pilate entered into the judgment hall again, and called Jesus, and said unto him, Art thou the King of the Jews?

34 Jesus answered him, Sayest thou this thing of thyself, or did others tell it thee of me?

35 Pilate answered, Am I a Jew? Thine own nation and the chief priests have delivered thee unto me: what hast thou done?

36 Jesus answered, My kingdom is not of this world: if my kingdom were of this world, then would my servants fight, that I should not be delivered to the Jews: but now is my kingdom not from hence.

37 Pilate therefore said unto him, Art thou a king then? Jesus answered, Thou sayest that I am a king. To this end was I born, and for this cause came I into the world, that I should bear witness unto the truth. Every one that is of the truth heareth my voice.

38 Pilate saith unto him, What is truth? And when he had said this, he went out again unto the Jews, and saith unto them, I find in him no fault at all.

***Pilate out to the Jews vv.28-32***

39 But ye have a custom, that I should release unto you one at the passover: will ye therefore that I release unto you the King of the Jews?

40 Then cried they all again, saying, Not this man, but Barabbas. Now Barabbas was a robber.

A.  Why did the Lord Jesus say "I Am" in the garden? v.5.

B.  How many times did Peter deny Christ? vv.12-27 (13.38).

C.  What charges were laid against Christ in His trial? vv.28-32.

D.  What is the answer to Pilate's question in v.38?

_________________________________________________

_________________________________________________

_________________________________________________

_________________________________________________

# John 19
**The Lord before Pilate 18.28 to 19.16**
*Pilate into the Judgment Hall vv.1-3*
1 Then Pilate therefore took Jesus, and scourged him.
2 And the soldiers platted a crown of thorns, and put it on his head, and they put on him a purple robe,
3 And said, Hail, King of the Jews! and they smote him with their hands.
*Pilate out to the Jews vv.4-7*
4 Pilate therefore went forth again, and saith unto them, Behold, I bring him forth to you, that ye may know that I find no fault in him.
5 Then came Jesus forth, wearing the crown of thorns, and the purple robe. And Pilate saith unto them, Behold the man!
6 When the chief priests therefore and officers saw him, they cried out, saying, Crucify him, crucify him. Pilate saith unto them, Take ye him, and crucify him: for I find no fault in him.
7 The Jews answered him, We have a law, and by our law he ought to die, because he made himself the Son of God.
*Pilate into the Judgment Hall vv.8-12*
8 When Pilate therefore heard that saying, he was the more afraid;
9 And went again into the judgment hall, and saith unto Jesus, Whence art thou? But Jesus gave him no answer.
10 Then saith Pilate unto him, Speakest thou not unto me? knowest thou not that I have power to crucify thee, and have power to release thee?
11 Jesus answered, Thou couldest have no power at all against me, except it were given thee from above: therefore he that delivered me unto thee hath the greater sin.
12 And from thenceforth Pilate sought to release him: but the Jews cried out, saying, If thou let this man go, thou art not Caesar's friend: whosoever maketh himself a king speaketh against Caesar.
*Pilate out to the Jews vv.13-16*
13 When Pilate therefore heard that saying, he brought Jesus forth, and sat down in the judgment seat in a place that is called the Pavement, but in the Hebrew, Gabbatha.
14 And it was the preparation of the passover, and about the sixth hour: and he saith unto the Jews, Behold your King!
15 But they cried out, Away with him, away with him,

---

19.3 'smote' means 'struck'.

19.4 'forth' means 'out'.
19.1-6 Pilate is trying to illicit sympathy through the intense sufferings and abuse given to the Christ. Pilate three times has announced that there was no fault in Christ (18.38; 19.4, 6). But the crowd is unmoved by His sufferings and cry out for His crucifixion. Emotion never saves.

19.7-8 The issue which caused the hatred and desire for His death as well as Pilate's great fear was His claim to be God the Son.

19.9 'Whence art thou?' means 'Where are you from?' The Lord was silent.
He had answered this already (18.33-37). He was the King from heaven.

19.11 Pilate is being told he is powerless!
19.11 'Greater sin' – the Lord is teaching that greater responsibility brings greater culpability and judgement. Caiaphas the High Priest does have a greater sin than Pilate. Pilate was acting within his delegated authority and wrongfully condemned and tortured an innocent man for which he will be held accountable. The High Priest was acting in the authority of God and he condemned the Christ of God to death for which he will be held eternally responsible.

crucify him. Pilate saith unto them, Shall I crucify your King? The chief priests answered, We have no king but Caesar.

16 Then delivered he him therefore unto them to be crucified. And they took Jesus, and led him away.

**The Crucifixion of the Lord and His Death 17-42**
*Pilate, the Soldiers and the Cross vv.17-24*

17 **And he bearing his cross went forth into a place called the place of a skull, which is called in the Hebrew Golgotha**:

18 **Where they crucified him, and two other with him, on either side one, and Jesus in the midst**.

19 And Pilate wrote a title, and put it on the cross. And the writing was Jesus Of Nazareth The King Of The Jews.

20 This title then read many of the Jews: for the place where Jesus was crucified was nigh to the city: and it was written in Hebrew, and Greek, and Latin.

21 Then said the chief priests of the Jews to Pilate, Write not, The King of the Jews; but that he said, I am King of the Jews.

22 Pilate answered, What I have written I have written.

23 Then the soldiers, when they had crucified Jesus, took his garments, and made four parts, to every soldier a part; and also his coat: now the coat was without seam, woven from the top throughout.

24 They said therefore among themselves, Let us not rend it, but cast lots for it, whose it shall be: that the scripture might be fulfilled, which saith, They parted my raiment among them, and for my vesture they did cast lots. These things therefore the soldiers did.

*The Women, and the Lord's Death vv.25-30*

25 Now there stood by the cross of Jesus his mother, and his mother's sister, Mary the wife of Cleophas, and Mary Magdalene.

26 When Jesus therefore saw his mother, and the disciple standing by, whom he loved, he saith unto his mother, Woman, behold thy son!

27 Then saith he to the disciple, Behold thy mother! And from that hour that disciple took her unto his own home.

28 After this, Jesus knowing that all things were now accomplished, that the scripture might be fulfilled, saith, I thirst.

29 Now there was set a vessel full of vinegar: and they filled a spunge with vinegar, and put it upon hyssop, and put it to his mouth.

30 **When Jesus therefore had received the vinegar, he said, It is finished: and he bowed his head, and gave up the ghost.**

---

19.13-16 Spiritual tension for Pilate's salvation was between Caesar or Christ? The same choice continues for all others afterwards (v16). Each need to ask, Who is our Caesar?

19.23 'garments' refers to his clothes worn under his coat.

19.24 'rend' means 'rip'.
'Lots' means to draw straws or throw dice.
'Fulfilled' – see psalm 22.18.

19.25 four loyal and devoted women – three of them called Mary.

19.29 'hyssop' – a small shrub/ plant often used for sprinkling.

19.31 'preparation' – the name the Jews gave to the day before the Feast of Unleavened Bread. Breaking legs hastens death by crucifixion as those being crucified cannot push themselves up for a breath and so they die for lack of oxygen.

19.34 Blood and water indicate that he was dead already. John had seen many dead people and knew the difference between the blood of a living man and a dead man. The thick red blood had clotted and coagulated and poured out with the liquid serum. John gives eye witness evidence for what he saw that proves the Lord really had died.

19.41 'sepulchre' means 'tomb', 'grave'.

### The Lord's Body Laid in a Sepulchre vv.31-42

31 The Jews therefore, because it was the preparation, that the bodies should not remain upon the cross on the sabbath day, (for that sabbath day was an high day,) besought Pilate that their legs might be broken, and that they might be taken away.

32 Then came the soldiers, and brake the legs of the first, and of the other which was crucified with him.

33 But when they came to Jesus, and saw that he was dead already, they brake not his legs:

34 But one of the soldiers with a spear pierced his side, and forthwith came there out blood and water.

35 And he that saw it bare record, and his record is true: and he knoweth that he saith true, that ye might believe.

36 For these things were done, that the scripture should be fulfilled, A bone of him shall not be broken.

37 And again another scripture saith, They shall look on him whom they pierced.

38 And after this Joseph of Arimathaea, being a disciple of Jesus, but secretly for fear of the Jews, besought Pilate that he might take away the body of Jesus: and Pilate gave him leave. He came therefore, and took the body of Jesus.

39 And there came also Nicodemus, which at the first came to Jesus by night, and brought a mixture of myrrh and aloes, about an hundred pound weight.

40 Then took they the body of Jesus, and wound it in linen clothes with the spices, as the manner of the Jews is to bury.

41 Now in the place where he was crucified there was a garden; and in the garden a new sepulchre, wherein was never man yet laid.

42 There laid they Jesus therefore because of the Jews' preparation day; for the sepulchre was nigh at hand.

A.  Why did the Jews want the Lord Jesus to die? v.7.

B.  Who was more important to Pilate than Christ? vv.12-16.

C.  What did the Psalmist prophecy concerning Christ 1,000 years before it happened? v.24.

D.  Why does John give us so much detail concerning the actual death of Christ? v.35.

_______________________________________

_______________________________________

_______________________________________

_______________________________________

# John 20
## Resurrection Manifestations in Jerusalem vv.1-31
### *Mary, Peter and John at the Sepulchre vv.1-10*

20.1 The stone must have been a considerable size as the woman worried how this stone might be removed for embalming the body (Mark 16.3).

20.3 that 'other disciple' – again this is John the disciple.

20.7-8 Eye witness testimony of incredible order. The linen clothes and the napkin that was around his head were lying as if the body had just risen through them, not thrown carelessly to one side by grave robbers.

20.9 'knew not the scripture' – not knowing is a theme in John's gospel. They had been told that He would rise again from the dead (John 1.10, 26; 2.9, 20.9,14; 21.4) but they had failed to believe the Lord's words.

20.14 'turned herself' -she was standing with her back to the Lord Jesus and she begins to turn around and in her peripheral vision she seems him but thinks it is the gardener.

20.15 'borne him hence' – means 'taken Him somewhere else'. 'Mary' – one word was enough to transform her life for ever. She saw a resurrected Christ.

1 The first day of the week cometh Mary Magdalene early, when it was yet dark, unto the sepulchre, and seeth the stone taken away from the sepulchre.
2 Then she runneth, and cometh to Simon Peter, and to the other disciple, whom Jesus loved, and saith unto them, They have taken away the Lord out of the sepulchre, and we know not where they have laid him.
3 Peter therefore went forth, and that other disciple, and came to the sepulchre.
4 So they ran both together: and the other disciple did outrun Peter, and came first to the sepulchre.
5 And he stooping down, and looking in, saw the linen clothes lying; yet went he not in.
6 Then cometh Simon Peter following him, and went into the sepulchre, and seeth the linen clothes lie,
7 And the napkin, that was about his head, not lying with the linen clothes, but wrapped together in a place by itself.
8 Then went in also that other disciple, which came first to the sepulchre, and he saw, and believed.
9 For as yet they knew not the scripture, that he must rise again from the dead.
10 Then the disciples went away again unto their own home.

### *The Lord with Mary in the Garden vv.11-18*

11 But Mary stood without at the sepulchre weeping: and as she wept, she stooped down, and looked into the sepulchre,
12 And seeth two angels in white sitting, the one at the head, and the other at the feet, where the body of Jesus had lain.
13 And they say unto her, Woman, why weepest thou? She saith unto them, Because they have taken away my Lord, and I know not where they have laid him.
14 And when she had thus said, she turned herself back, and saw Jesus standing, and knew not that it was Jesus.
15 Jesus saith unto her, Woman, why weepest thou? whom seekest thou? She, supposing him to be the gardener, saith unto him, Sir, if thou have borne him hence, tell me where thou hast laid him, and I will take him away.
16 Jesus saith unto her, Mary. She turned herself, and saith unto him, Rabboni; which is to say, Master.

17 Jesus saith unto her, Touch me not; for I am not yet ascended to my Father: but go to my brethren, and say unto them, I ascend unto my Father, and your Father; and to my God, and your God.

18 Mary Magdalene came and told the disciples that she had seen the Lord, and that he had spoken these things unto her.

### The Lord with the Apostles in the Upper Room vv.19-31

19 Then the same day at evening, being the first day of the week, when the doors were shut where the disciples were assembled for fear of the Jews, came Jesus and stood in the midst, and saith unto them, Peace be unto you.

20 And when he had so said, he shewed unto them his hands and his side. Then were the disciples glad, when they saw the Lord.

21 Then said Jesus to them again, Peace be unto you: as my Father hath sent me, even so send I you.

22 And when he had said this, he breathed on them, and saith unto them, Receive ye the Holy Ghost:

23 Whose soever sins ye remit, they are remitted unto them; and whose soever sins ye retain, they are retained.

24 But Thomas, one of the twelve, called Didymus, was not with them when Jesus came.

25 The other disciples therefore said unto him, We have seen the Lord. But he said unto them, Except I shall see in his hands the print of the nails, and put my finger into the print of the nails, and thrust my hand into his side, I will not believe.

26 And after eight days again his disciples were within, and Thomas with them: then came Jesus, the doors being shut, and stood in the midst, and said, Peace be unto you.

27 Then saith he to Thomas, Reach hither thy finger, and behold my hands; and reach hither thy hand, and thrust it into my side: and be not faithless, but believing.

28 And Thomas answered and said unto him, My Lord and my God.

29 Jesus saith unto him, Thomas, because thou hast seen me, thou hast believed: blessed are they that have not seen, and yet have believed.

30 And many other signs truly did Jesus in the presence of his disciples, which are not written in this book:

31 **But these are written, that ye might believe that Jesus is the Christ, the Son of God; and that believing ye might have life through his name.**

20.17 'Touch me not' - His relationship with His disciples is now entirely spiritual.

20.23 'Remit/remitted' means 'forgive/forgiven'.

20.28 The unbelieving Thomas falls before Christ and takes Him as His Lord and God when He sees Him in resurrection. He does not require the evidence of touch but accepts His word. It is no different to receive salvation today. We accept His word.

20.29 All who come to believe in the resurrected Jesus Christ are eternally blessed.

20.31 The reason John wrote His gospel is that you might be a believer in the Lord Jesus Christ, the Son of God and receive everlasting life. Have you believed?

# *Reflective Questions and Notes*

A. Who won the race to the tomb after Mary told them the stone was rolled away? v.4.

B. Who did Mary initially think the Lord Jesus was? v.15.

C. What did Thomas say was required before he would believe in a resurrected Christ? v.25.

D. Why did John write this Gospel? v.31.

# John 21

## Resurrection Manifestations in Galilee vv.1-25
### *The Eighth Sign: The Lord's Provision in Service vv.1-14*

1 After these things Jesus shewed himself again to the disciples at the sea of Tiberias; and on this wise shewed he himself.

2 There were together Simon Peter, and Thomas called Didymus, and Nathanael of Cana in Galilee, and the sons of Zebedee, and two other of his disciples.

3 Simon Peter saith unto them, I go a fishing. They say unto him, We also go with thee. They went forth, and entered into a ship immediately; and that night they caught nothing.

4 But when the morning was now come, Jesus stood on the shore: but the disciples knew not that it was Jesus.

5 Then Jesus saith unto them, Children, have ye any meat? They answered him, No.

6 And he said unto them, Cast the net on the right side of the ship, and ye shall find. They cast therefore, and now they were not able to draw it for the multitude of fishes.

7 Therefore that disciple whom Jesus loved saith unto Peter, It is the Lord. Now when Simon Peter heard that it was the Lord, he girt his fisher's coat unto him, (for he was naked,) and did cast himself into the sea.

8 And the other disciples came in a little ship; (for they were not far from land, but as it were two hundred cubits,) dragging the net with fishes.

9 As soon then as they were come to land, they saw a fire of coals there, and fish laid thereon, and bread.

10 Jesus saith unto them, Bring of the fish which ye have now caught.

11 Simon Peter went up, and drew the net to land full of great fishes, an hundred and fifty and three: and for all there were so many, yet was not the net broken.

12 Jesus saith unto them, Come and dine. And none of the disciples durst ask him, Who art thou? knowing that it was the Lord.

13 Jesus then cometh, and taketh bread, and giveth them, and fish likewise.

14 This is now the third time that Jesus shewed himself to his disciples, after that he was risen from the dead.

---

21.1 'shewed' means 'manifested'. The 'Sea of Tiberias' is another name for the sea of Galilee.

21.5 'have ye any meat?' means 'do you have anything to eat?'.

21.1-7 How this must have reminded them of their call some three years earlier when he told them he would make them fishers of men (Luke 5.1-11).

21.7 'disciple whom Jesus loved' – John was also on the boat as one of the seven (see v2).

21.8 'naked' does not mean nude. It means he did not have his outer coat on.

'200 cubits' – just under 100 metres.

21.12 'come and dine' means 'come and have breakfast'; 'Durst ask him' means 'did inquire from him'.

21.15 'dined' means 'eaten'.

21.18 'girdest' means 'clothed'.

21.19 The Lord was telling Peter he would live to an old life but his final hour would be not in his control. Peter died a martyr's death.

21.20 'disciple whom Jesus loved' – this was John the disciple. John always held special the fact that Jesus loved him. So should we all.

21.23 The Lord held out the possibility that some disciples would never die as He was coming back again. John did not know if he was going to be in that category. One day the Lord Jesus will return as He promised (John 14.1-3). The believers alive at that time will never have to pass through the article of death but will be immediately transformed (1Cor. 15.51-57).

21.25 John is saying the theme of his Gospel is inexhaustible. By the Spirit of God he selected some of the sayings and signs of Christ in order that we might believe that Jesus is the Christ, the Son of God and have everlasting life (20.31). After trusting Him as Saviour and Lord there is so much more to know.

### *Peter's Love vv.15-17*

15 So when they had dined, Jesus saith to Simon Peter, Simon, son of Jonas, lovest thou me more than these? He saith unto him, Yea, Lord; thou knowest that I love thee. He saith unto him, Feed my lambs.

16 He saith to him again the second time, Simon, son of Jonas, lovest thou me? He saith unto him, Yea, Lord; thou knowest that I love thee. He saith unto him, Feed my sheep.

17 He saith unto him the third time, Simon, son of Jonas, lovest thou me? Peter was grieved because he said unto him the third time, Lovest thou me? And he said unto him, Lord, thou knowest all things; thou knowest that I love thee. Jesus saith unto him, Feed my sheep.

### *The Apostles' Future Foretold vv.18-25*

18 Verily, verily, I say unto thee, When thou wast young, thou girdest thyself, and walkedst whither thou wouldest: but when thou shalt be old, thou shalt stretch forth thy hands, and another shall gird thee, and carry thee whither thou wouldest not.

19 This spake he, signifying by what death he should glorify God. And when he had spoken this, he saith unto him, Follow me.

20 Then Peter, turning about, seeth the disciple whom Jesus loved following; which also leaned on his breast at supper, and said, Lord, which is he that betrayeth thee?

21 Peter seeing him saith to Jesus, Lord, and what shall this man do?

22 Jesus saith unto him, If I will that he tarry till I come, what is that to thee? follow thou me.

23 Then went this saying abroad among the brethren, that that disciple should not die: yet Jesus said not unto him, He shall not die; but, If I will that he tarry till I come, what is that to thee?

24 This is the disciple which testifieth of these things, and wrote these things: and we know that his testimony is true.

25 And there are also many other things which Jesus did, the which, if they should be written every one, I suppose that even the world itself could not contain the books that should be written. Amen.

# *Reflective Questions and Notes*

A.  What would the experience in the boat remind the disciples of? vv.1-12.

B.  How would we answer the question the Lord asked Peter? vv.15,16,17.

C.  What promise did all the disciples believe was a possibility in their lifetime? vv.22,23.

D.  What was the last command He gave to His disciples? vv.19,22.

_____________________________________

_____________________________________

_____________________________________

_____________________________________